From the ~~Shenandoah~~ Valley and Beyond with God

Edition II

Roy Pierce

outskirtspress

DENVER, COLORADO

From The Unadilla Valley And Beyond With God
Edition II
All Rights Reserved.
Copyright © 2016 Roy Pierce
v2.0

Outskirts Press, Inc.
http://www.outskirtspress.com

ISBN: 978-1-4787-7523-2

Outskirts Press and the "OP" logo are trademarks belonging to Outskirts Press, Inc.

PRINTED IN THE UNITED STATES OF AMERICA

Table of Contents

ACKNOWLEDGEMENT

I would like to express my thanks to God for His love mercy and grace, and for my Savior Jesus Christ. Without Him, I would be lost. Praise God! I am saved and on my way to Heaven.

I would also like to thank my wife Patti, the mother of my five children. My family is a very supportive family. We became quite close while serving in the Philippines as missionaries. Patti and the children were with me through the many trials and tribulations of church planting ministry. They have continued their support through all the health issues since returning to the States.

I would also like to thank my parents (now deceased) who raised me in a Christian home and taught me the importance of worshipping Christ in church and instilling in me godly values. My wife, and her parents (also deceased), played a huge role in my Christian heritage as well.

I also want to thank God for the farms where I was a boarder from age 13 through out my High School years. There were three farms where I boarded from age thirteen to graduation from High School. The Miller farms in Earlville, New York; The Leo Johnson farm in West Edmeston, New York; and the Clyde Head farm of Waterville, New York. In the last three months of my senior year of high school, I ran the Ogden farm in Waterville, New York. He had to stop milking his cows. He developed ulcers on his arms. Plus, he was quite busy with his saw-mill business.

Also thank you to many, many friends and acquaintances that I have made along my journey from Unadilla Valley in central New York, across the continental United States, to the Philippine Islands and back. I have served in our Home Church; Mission work; Christian Education and two Pastorate positions; Senior Citizens ministry at the Buford Road Baptist Church as their leader in Richmond, Virginia. They are a special group of God's people that Patti and I have really enjoyed getting to know and love in the Lord. I also spent a few years peer counseling and a Chaplain's assistant at the local Veterans Administration Hospital, in Richmond, Virginia working in the spinal cord unit. Being a paralyzed veteran helps me to relate to them well. It also gave me a ministry at that time. Since then I have become well enough to help do fair ministry with the Amazing Grace Mission. Patti and I (with the help of others) set up a booth at Fairs & Festivals. We share the gospel and sometimes council with many people. It is a great way to help people in our retirement years.

*** *I am editing this in September 2013.* ***

I can only praise God for 45 years of faithful service to Him. If it were not for health issues, I would still be serving Him full time. God knows my heart and has seen fit for me to share Christ and encourage others for now.

I would like to thank my wife Patti and my oldest daughter Patsy for taking the time to help proof read my manuscript for me. They have done an excellent job!

I dedicate this book to my wonderful wife Patti and
my five great children: Patsy, Troy, Carla, Kandi, and Jason. Also to the many Pastors, and friends, and other missionaries in Christ who gave of their time to help me become a servant of God.

The book that you will be reading is what I remember to the best of my ability.

1

BORN IN THE UNADILLA VALLEY

I am not sure how many of my readers would even know where the Unadilla Valley is located.

It is in Central New York State, in the region stemming south of Utica, New York, and ends near Binghamton, New York. It is along the U.S. Route 8 corridor. It is a beautiful quiet area of the country. It has a river running through most of it and is comprised mostly of dairy farms and small towns. Each morning and evening, there was a steam locomotive train that went up and down the valley bringing supplies to these towns. This was the area of my birth and God had a special reason for my life!

Hello! My name is Le "Roy" D. Pierce and I was born in one such small town named Leonardsville, New York, located about twelve miles south of Utica, New York. The year was 1941 and it was December 9th 1941, just two days after the bombing of Pearl Harbor. My dad was a share crop farmer working on one of the Welch farms known as the Button Falls farms, located about three miles south of Leonardsville, New York. Arthur Welch owned two farms one right on route 8, and the other one up in the hollow. He and his wife, Edna, had two boys and two girls. Charlie Welch was my age and Clayton was two years younger. The two girls, Elrina and Lucille, were older.

Life was simple back then. My parents, Harry & Etta Pierce, went once a month to the Watkins General Store, (owned by Mr. Watkins) and Dad would get a hair cut around the corner in the Barber Shop. Mom went there often to visit with the barber's wife, who happened to be the mid-wife for many folks in the area. One cold December day, while Dad was getting his hair cut and Mom was in talking with the mid-wife, I happened to want to come into the world. Yes, I was born right there in the side room of the old Barbershop on December 9, 1941.

My earliest memories were of the "little old country home on route 8." We had a kitchen stove on which Mom cooked. Hot water was available in the reserve tank on the side of the stove. One of the things that this hot water was used for was to be dipped into the washtub on Saturday nights for our bath.

Another thing was, Mom kept a rind from the bacon on a nail behind the wood stove. She used it to grease the fry pan or the griddle. She would also keep a can of milk there if and when it had been rejected from the milk station for some reason or another. After a few days, when the milk was sour and had thick "globs" in it, she would make a batch of home-made cottage cheese. The best I have ever had!

There was a cast Iron which was laid on the back of the stove to heat for ironing clothes or to wrap in a towel and be placed inside the blankets by my feet in the winter. Winters were cold and I welcomed the warmth. That old wood stove also kept many new born piglets warm in the winter. Dad would place them in a wood box behind the stove on cold wintry nights.

There also was a round Cherry Chunk stove in the living room to keep that part of the house semi-warm. The top of that stove had a flat surface. Mom always kept a large pan of water there that served as our humidifier (or more hot water when needed). Both of the stoves, of course, used wood - a lot of wood! I loved going in the woods to get wood! The woods are so filled with the presence of God.

I really enjoyed playing and exploring the outdoors. Back then, and as I previously mentioned, a train went up through the valley each morning. In fact, it went right up the tracks at the end of our cow pasture. Back then trains burned coal and the puffs of smoke were fun to watch.

The Unadilla River also went down through the pastureland. This became a good place to catch frogs and turtles. Frogs were for frog legs and the rest went to the turtles. The frog legs made good eating! Also, the turtles were for turtle soup. I remember finding a rather large turtle one afternoon and having my dad help get it after our chores. He had a barn broom and a large washtub. I was excited until I saw the turtle snap the brooms handle in half very fast! We decided to let it be since it was a big snapping turtle.

As I got a little older, I liked to be around the working process of the farm. My dad got me my first pair of rubber boots when I was five. I still remember that moment even today. Each morning dad would bring the horses and wagon into the barn. On each side of the floor were gutters that we needed to shovel. Dad would stand on one side and I would be on the other. I took hold of a barn shovel and tried to help shovel out manure from the gutter without splashing Dad on the other side. I was too short, however, to throw the shovels-full up into the wagon. When Dad drove the horses and wagon out to the field I could help a lot easier. (It is always easier to throw out and down rather than up and over). It was fun when Dad showed me how to take the shovel or the dung fork full and sling your hand as you threw so that it would spread. It was quite an act to do so properly, and boy was I really enjoying my new rubber boots!

One of my favorite things was just being around the horses. The horses were big, but they did not seem to mind this boy much. Maybe it was because I put oats in their feed trough. I liked old "Jack" and "Duke". They were beautiful Strawberry Rhone horses.

One day, Dad had hooked them up to the sulky plow and was plowing. I would walk behind them watching the earth turn over to collect worms for fishing. I was beginning to understand a bit of what farming was all about. The next day Dad only took Jack and hooked him up to a furrow plow. He said that he needed to plow the ends of the field. However, before he started he got Duke, and hooked him up to the drag and then asked me to bring Duke behind him into the field. This was fun!

When we arrived at the field, he took Duke in just a bit and pulled the handle back on the drag. He then had me stand on the back brace of the drag and hold the lines. I clicked my cheeks and Duke took off walking. Now I was dragging the field! When I was just about to the end, Duke began to turn and went over a few yards and we headed back to the other end. (Now, you realize that a trained horse already knows what to do, but this sure was exciting)! I spent all day going back and forth. About 4:30 p.m. Dad came and took over since one of my regular jobs was to go to the pasture and get the cows headed down to the barn for milking. Dad also headed for the barn a short time later.

While Dad was milking, I swept out the mangers, then climbed up into the silo and threw down silage until it was almost up to the silo shoot. After that, I came down and I also helped feed silage to the cows with an old washtub. I then scraped off the area behind the cows and put sawdust down. After that, I would sweep the silage back up to the cows so they could finish eating. (For a young boy it all was not perfect.), but I helped!

My next chore was taking pails of water and scoops of oats to the horses in their stalls. In the summertime when the milking was completely finished, I would let the cows out to the pasture again. In the winter, we would put hay down for them and leave them in the barn. This was hard work for a little boy who did all he could to help. It kept me out of trouble and I enjoyed it. God's goodness was all around on the farm!

Back in those days, suppertime around the table was always fun. The family sat together sharing the day's events. Usually we ate homemade corn bread or biscuits, mashed potatoes, canned beef or pork and vegetables that mom had canned herself. Sometimes we ended the meal with gingerbread topped with homemade whipped cream, or simply cookies. It all was so good! In the winter, we made homemade ice cream which was also really good!

After the supper meal, we had family devotions. Dad would read, from the Bible and Mom would read from the Daily Bread. We prayed together and then off we would go to play for a short time before we went to bed.

Even-though we lived just a few yards from the road (Route 8), back then hardly anyone drove by at night. It was quiet on the farm at night!

The next morning after the chores were finished we ate our breakfast. Breakfast most often was oatmeal, corn muffins, or biscuits with maple syrup. I followed Dad up to the shed behind the barn. That was where he kept cobs of corn. He would take one cob at a time and put it in the hole on the side of this big wheel that he spun with his foot. The cob of corn would go down the hole that slanting into the wheel. The wheel had rows of little pegs on it and as the wheel turned, the pegs would shell off the kernels of corn. After he had about three pails of shelled corn, Dad poured them in a large tub with some black tar. He stirred this strange mixture together well. I asked him what the tar was for and he told me that when you planted the corn this way, the crows would not dig it up and eat it. I learned years later that tar was outlawed.

After lunch, which usually consisted of soup and peanut butter sandwich, I followed Dad back up to the barn where he harnessed the horses. He then went over to the shed and hooked them up to the corn planter. After pouring the corn into the two hoppers on the planter, he headed to the field. Next he pulled the lever back and the planter lowered into the soft dirt. It was soft because the field had been plowed, and also dragged. If it was new sod ground it also needed disking. Thus, Dad began planting corn. My job in the process was to pick up any stones that might be in the way of the corn furrows. One did not want any stones in the way of the sprouting corn or later during the harvest season. Soon, 4:30 came and it was chore time once-again. Another day was finished in corn planting, which usually took 3-4 days total.

There was also a field that had been prepared for planting oats. It was on this field dad walked along with a bag of wheat. He put his hand in the bag, got some wheat and as he threw the wheat, he opened his fingers in the process. This spread the wheat thinly over the ground. This is how he planted the oats and wheat. God would make it grow.

The next day was different. Dad harnessed the horses and I trailed him back out to the shed where he hooked them up to the hay mower. The mower had two steel wheels with lugs on them. This allowed the wheels to grab the ground while being pulled forward by the horses. There was a sickle bar with guards and a long thin sickle with knives that went back and forth through the guards cutting the hay as the machine moved forward. I noticed that Dad brought a pitchfork along with him and I soon realized what it was to be used for. The hay was high, and the swath-board on the end of the sickle-bar would have too much hay to turn over and this hay fell back in the way of mowing.

My job was to use the pitchfork to pick up the hay moving it back out way of the next swath to be cut. Then when Dad came back around with the mower, the mower would not clog. I did not think this was a fun job at all! The biggest reason was that every so often the mower would stir up a nest of bees. Although my Dad said, "Son, remain quiet and relaxed", it was hard not to be nervous! I learned that our body gives off a chemical, when we are excited, and that is when the bees attack. I was actually relieved when 4:30 came around so I could go get the cows for milking time!

It rained during that night and Dad was concerned about the fresh-cut hay. It was not good for fresh-cut hay to get wet. It took some of the goodness out of it. It did stop raining around 10:00 that day, and the sun came out. I really cannot remember much else about that particular day. I probably played around in the hayloft killing pigeons. The barn cats sure liked them and I thought the pigeon breast meat was tasty as Mom cooked them up for us to eat. I do remember the following day though as long as I live.

The following day, the fresh-cut hay that had gotten wet was beginning to dry out and needed some attention. Dad gathered up the bosses' two sons, Charlie, and Clayton and I. Then we all walked to the field with a pitchfork in our hands. Each of the swaths of hay had to be turned upside down, no other way but by hand! We went around the field and back all day until it was chore time. Charlie and Clayton finished the job while Dad and I did chores in the barn. I am sure glad the fields were a lot smaller then! God gives us strength for the job though.

I do not remember too much until a few days later. There was something different in the air as I awoke that particular morning. Mom was putting dishes, as well as pots and pans in boxes. She needed my help. I asked her what was happening and she told me that they needed Dad to run the farm up in the hollow. This was nice since it was up in the hollow very near the Button Falls. I had been up there before. Dad would take us up there for a picnic and to swim on days off or holidays. There was a nice large pool of water under the falls. I remember that it was deep enough for Dad to climb about twenty feet or so and jump off into the pool.

If we were to move up there wow! It was nice man! The cool shade from the trees and the flowing waterfalls was a special place.

Each year about this time brought me good memories of the "Wigdens." Gladys was the piano player and the two brothers sang and preached revival meetings! They stayed with Arthur & Edna Welch. Bob was the big man and loved to plow the field. He said that it reminded him of when a person is saved and God has opened up new life! God sure has made some wonderful places and people for us to enjoy! However, a new chapter is about to unfold.

2

THE UPPER FALLS FARM

What a different day this was! Dad left early with the boss and headed to Madison, New York. My job was to help Mom load the wagon that Dad had backed up to the woodshed. He had tied the horses and put some hay down for them to eat. Mom showed me what boxes and things I could carry for her. We put as much on the wagon as we could, and then gathered the rest of our belongings to store in the woodshed until later.

I did not realize the reason that dad had gone with the boss to Madison, New York. Boy was I surprised when he drove into our driveway with a brand-new 1946 Dodge pickup truck! He was to use the truck to go to and from the two farms. It came in handy for many of the farm jobs that took a long time with horses. Not only that, we used the truck to go to church I don't remember going before, and we used the pickup to go to the grocery store. We also got vacation time since Dad's boss gave him one week a year and we could use the truck! Dad wanted to visit his brother, my Uncle Mike for our first vacation. We went to see his stepmother. Uncle Mike lived in Canandaigua, New York, and Grandma lived in Rochester, New York. I did not know my grandfather, but I remember that they had moved him, into the city of Rochester, New York, from the Indian reservation. He was a half-breed of the Iroquois nation. That made dad a quarter-breed, and me one sixteenth of an Indian! The reservation is located up near the Niagara Falls, North Tonawanda area of western New York.

Then I had another surprise!! Remember the new pickup I mentioned? Dad told me that while he and Mom loaded the pickup truck, I was to take the horses and wagon, and go through the pasture to the upper falls farm and wait. We were moving to a new home! WOW, this was surely a fun day! I took my time and enjoyed every moment.

Actually, the only way this could happen at my young age was the fact that the horses knew the way very well. The wagon was a rough-ride, and the household goods were delicate. However, I made it.

The new farmhouse was bigger than our old house. I failed to mention before this that I have two sisters; Jessie and Dorothy, who are both younger than I. Now they have their own bedroom I had one to myself! There were two bedrooms upstairs and Dad & Mom had their bedroom downstairs. However, the best was the "out-house" our toilet! We had a "one-hole" out house before; but this one had a two-hole seat! Now, for you who do not fully understand, the outhouse was the toilet. Usually there was a deep hole dug in the ground with a shed built over the top of the hole. Inside the shed, there was a frame, built. A wide board would then be placed, on the top of the frame. Then in this board, two holes were cut out, to sit on. Our toilet paper back in those days was usually an old Sears catalogue or some corncobs. There was never any water in these out houses.

The woodshed was huge, and the icebox was even bigger than our old one! The icebox was where we kept the milk and other food cool. There was a garage, also a tool shed built over an embankment, which allowed a hog pen underneath. There was even a nice chicken house, although the chickens ran around wild most of the time. Dad told me that this keeps them from getting fat. Chickens also fertilize the ground; and eat bugs, mosquitoes, and worms. As they dig and scratch the dirt for worms, chickens keep the ground in the garden loose. In the winter when the chickens stayed in the chicken house it got noisy at night sometimes when a fox or mink would get in there and try to get a chicken. Next to the chicken house were six juicy apple trees.

These apple trees kept the deer coming. It was fun to watch the deer in the apple orchard.

Down by the new barn was an old icehouse with a sawdust pen. We used sawdust under the cows when they were in the barn to keep them cleaner. I am telling you, for a young boy, this was a very nice farm!

Mom and Dad arrived with the loaded pickup. Now it was time to take everything I could into the house, while Mom and Dad brought in the bigger things. We had a good share of wagon unloaded when it turned 4:30 chore time! The barn was new to us with eighteen cows. The cows had been delivered by truck from the Welch's livestock farm in West Edmeston, New York. The Welch's had a farm auction that sold cows to many farmers in the area. They also brought us our own team of nice workhorses, a black one named Dan and a brown one named Molly. Dad started the milking and I put down some hay since there was no silage in the silo yet. After I finished putting down the hay, Dad told me to take Jack and Duke, our old team of horses, back down to the main farm. I would be doing this many times as all farmers helped one another back in those days.

My dad had finished the milking by the time I got back home while Mom had made us pancakes for supper. I had worked up an appetite after this busy day. After supper, it was time for Dad and Mom to put beds together while I went outside to the water well and pumped some water from the "pitcher pump." Yes! That is how we used to get our water. I always made sure there was a can of water left on the ledge. This was used to prime the pump the next time you needed water. I was exhausted! I fell asleep as soon as my head hit the pillow!

The next morning started a new routine. School had started for another year. My sisters and I got ready and walked about a quarter mile to the bus stop. There was only one stop on our old dirt road. All the children from the four farms waited for the bus at the same place. I noticed the bus coming! It was a new Reo Bus with our school (Leonardsville Central School) painted on it.

I did not mind school back then. Maybe they were carefree days of childhood. One thing for sure was that my lunchbox was, always filled with good things like leftover pancakes or biscuits with peanut butter, corn bread, or a baked bean sandwich, the simple leftover from supper the night before! The School was one big room with at least three different classes in it. We did not worry about wearing the wrong clothes, or fitting in because every student there was from a farm. The only exception was Barbara. She was the daughter of the local doctor. Doctor Evans happened to be the rural area Doctor. He was the only one around.

A normal class day began with the Pledge of Allegiance to the flag, and then prayer. Once in awhile we would be allowed to sing. Back in those day's you would also find a Gideon New Testament placed on your desk each year. There would also be a trial size of toothpaste.

One thing I must say is that if you happened to be caught whispering, or not paying attention, you would have to go up in front of the class, and hold out your hand. The teacher would slap your hand three times with the ruler. The embarrassment was worse than the punishment! I am here to tell you that you did not want to grab that ruler! You were then, introduced to the principal. The teacher would also put a note about the incident in your lunchbox for your parents to read. My dad would spank me again if Mom found a note in my lunchbox from the teacher.

After school, each day was chore time. That meant bringing the firewood into the house and piling it up behind each of the two stoves for the night, and then going to the barn for the regular chores. Dad would let the cows out so they could go down to the creek for a drink. After they drank, I would drive them back into the barn and lead the horses, one at a time, down to the creek to drink. In the winter, when the creek had frozen over, I would have to take the axe down with me to chop a hole in the ice for the cows or horses, so they could drink.

Another thing about the winter ice was when the neighbors got together and took the bobsleds with horses down to the river. The men would cut a hole in the ice with a long drill. Then they would take a short, crosscut saw and cut big blocks of ice. They then would put these big blocks of ice onto the bobsleds, which the horses pulled up to the sawdust shed. The blocks of ice were then, taken to the icehouse where they would be packed into the sawdust. This would keep them frozen. Ice, was what we used in the milk house to keep the milk cold. It also was cut in pieces, and brought into the woodshed, and placed in the icebox to keep our food cold. As you can tell, there were many things to keep you busy and no time to get into mischief or trouble. It is too bad that this is not the case these days! Life was simple, fun and busy, yet I loved it! Those years of growing up taught us values and lessons which molded us into what God would have us to become. I do want to thank God for those past years!! I wish that all young boys today could have the opportunity to work like this. There would not be the crime that we have today. It would keep them busy and they would not have so much free time on their hands. To be very truthful about it, it was not what you call today work. It was enjoyable tasks really! We did the work and enjoyed the blessings of what God gave back in return.

3

WINTERS IN THE HOLLOW

Winters, in the hollow were brutal! We lived right in the gap of the hollow. That meant the snow blew right up against the house and barn. I remember one particular morning that Dad was up in my room opening the window. He began moving the snow with the old shovel that we stored in the wood shed. I soon realized that the snow was all the way up past the kitchen windows, and up past our woodshed door. He finally jumped out the upstairs window into the snow and all I could see, was his head and the shovel whipping up the snow. (My dad was 6' 2") I watched while he would tunnel out snow, and then throw it up over the bank, then, knock down some more snow. After he finally made a path and got the woodshed door open, I was able to go out. The problem was all the other shovels were out in the barn. It was not long before I saw Dad begin to walk through the snow, as it was not so deep out away from the house and in the driveway. I was able to follow in the path that he made and we arrived at the barn. It was late for the chores, but they had to be, done. I did as much as I could before leaving for school. After waiting for the bus to come, Mom came and told us that school was probably, closed. We did not have official local news, back then. I agreed with Mom's decision as I looked up the road. The road that went past our house went up a steep hill. I can remember that the Town of Brookfield did finally come with the "Old Lynn,"

which was a monster of a snowplow. It had a very high V-type blade with bulldozer like tracks on it. Sometimes they came by with a giant snow blower that had two augers, one on top the other, to move the big high banks of snow. In fact, the road looked like a tunnel with the snow banks so high you could not see over either side of the road. Then on the right of the farm was a big knoll that used to fill in with a lot of snow, as well. As the snow melted during the day, it left us with ice in front of our driveway. The driveway was uphill leading to the barn and garage. I can remember many times Dad coming up the driveway with the pickup, spinning all the way. The tires back then were nylon and knobby tread. As the tires spun, they actually sounded like they were singing. Sometimes we would have to get the horses harnessed and come out to pull the truck up the driveway. FUN! FUN! FUN!

One of the things that Dad used to do to keep the wind from coming through the stone foundation of the house was a bit unusual. He would build a form around the house about three feet high by two feet wide. He then filled this with horse manure. It froze and really did not bother anything until spring when it really stunk!

I mentioned before about the old "cast-iron" that Mom used for clothes. It was always, on the back of the wood-stove keeping warm. On cold winter nights Mom would wrap a towel around it and place it inside the blankets down by our feet. It was nice and warm to go to sleep with, the iron and the old heavy horse blanket, made it cozy. I remember many mornings when I woke up there was some snow on the old blanket. The snow had come in through the old windowpanes. These old windowpanes had open cracks around the windows. I especially remember my younger cousin Dominick coming to spend a few nights with us. He was a few years younger than I and I picked on him a little. He slept in my room. When it was moonlight, you could see through the cracks and out into the apple orchard. I would have him look through the cracks of the old windowpanes, and see the limbs moving on the trees. I would tell him that they were monsters, coming to get him. He would dive under the blankets quite scared. He would also get scared because of the noise of the mice and squirrels over head in the ceiling.

I don't know how many of you that remember he old Black Walnut trees? Well, mom kept black walnuts up in the attic. She would crack these black walnuts open for Christmas cookies. Black walnuts did make good cookies and cake. The squirrels and mice however, liked to roll them around during the night.

On Saturdays, in the winters I would help Dad with the crosscut saw. That meant that he would be on one end pushing and my job was to push it back. Usually that meant cutting down one or two trees in the morning and trimming the branches. Then, after lunch, we would cut up the small limbs and branches. I usually tried to do much of this while Dad took the horses and the front section of the bobsled to pull the main logs up to the side of the house. The wagon that was used most of the time was on wheels, and the same box was put on a set of bobs with runners (like sleds) for the snow. After he finished pulling the trees up to the house, we would put the wagon box back on the bobsled and we would fill it with the limbs, and head back to the house. After we unloaded the limbs and branches, it was time for chores again. Always chores! It was always the same routine... 4:30 everyday.

The next day was Sunday! This meant that after breakfast, mom got some hot water out of the reservoir on the end of the kitchen, stove. She put the hot water in a tub with some cold water, and then came, a good-old fashion bath. In my bedroom, as I would be getting dressed, I could hear (every Sunday morning) Dad playing the radio. He liked to listen to Polka music. I would put on my clean pants, my only white dress shirt, and my only pair of shoes. I was then ready for Sunday school and church. Later in the week was Christmas! The day we celebrate Christ's birth!

Christmas in the hollow was exciting! There were many homemade decorations like popcorn that we would thread and make a popcorn rope for the tree. There were also macaroni decorations that Mom and her sister, my aunt Carol made. (Do not laugh...I thought, that they were nice!) Mom also had an angel that went on top of the tree and the pretty, big, balls of different colors, and five of the bubbling light bulbs, and lastly the regular lights. They were big light bulbs then, but if one blew, the rest stayed lit. We never put Christmas lights outside of our house. Instead, we had a candle light in each window of the house. Christmas evening I came in from chores and my Aunt Doris and Uncle Cliff had come to visit. I remember, as if it was yesterday, that after supper Aunt Doris gave me a present. It was a beautiful Children's story Bible. She showed me the plan of salvation and how I could become a Christian. I can still remember it clearly. I kept that book for a long time, and shared it with Patsy, our oldest daughter, and Troy our son.

On Christmas morning, after the chores, we opened our stockings. The stockings were filled with a small coloring book or a puzzle book. Sometimes we got a used comic book from the Welch boys. There would be homemade candy and a caramel popcorn ball. Each of us got one orange, and we were not, allowed to throw the orange rinds away. Mom gathered them all and put them in a fry pan, to make orange rind candy. It was what you might call "bitter-sweet" candy, but it was good!

Early afternoon Lawrence and Ann Baldwin would arrive. They were friends (farmers) that Dad and Mom knew and helped, for a long time. They did not have children. They were however, good friends of our family. We always shared Christmas with them. After lunch, we would open our presents. My sisters and I only got one present, as times were hard. I always got a white shirt to wear Sundays, for as long as I can remember. Lawrence and Ann would give us a gift such as a toy truck, or a pair of socks or mittens. These were good times. We would pick up the wrappings, and bows, trying to save as much of it as possible as it would be used again sometime. Just before chore time, we would all gather around to sing "Happy Birthday" to Jesus, and have dessert. Usually we had a birthday cake for Jesus, suet pudding and homemade pies such as: blackberry, mincemeat, or apple, but who cared, as they were all good!

In mid February each year, for about six weeks we had the "sugar bush" season. I would go with Dad into the woods and helped carry the spiles. Dad had a large hand augur drill with him. When we found a maple tree, he would drill into the tree twice, maybe three times if the tree happened to be large. My job was to use the wooden mallet and drive the spiles into the holes. There was a small hole in the end of the spile and three slits. The hole and slits in the spile allowed sap to flow out of the tree and into the bucket. On each of the spiles, we hung a bucket, in which collected the sap.

The next step in the process was to put a big vat on the bobsled. Then the horses pulled the bobsled down into the woods. At this point, we emptied the buckets of sap into the vat. Dad collected the sap after the morning chores. Then he hauled the sap to the yard near the woodshed, where there was a long narrow thin vat over a fire. Then we would boil the sap down into maple syrup. If I remember correctly, It took forty gallons of sap to make one gallon of maple syrup. That is a lot of sap! I was able to help collect the sap after school in the afternoons. After the chores were done, and as the sap was boiling down, we would drop some of the hot sap into the snow and it became a sort of candy. Mmm! Good! The final stage of boiling the sap then would be handed over to Mom to finish off on the kitchen wood stove. Maple sugar and maple syrup was favorites for us on the farm. It was actually our sugar supply, and our syrup for biscuits and pancakes. We all really liked it!

As spring came and the weather turned warmer, the plowing, and mending fences began. We had to mend fences because of the heavy winter snow that broke down fence posts and wires. Sometimes tree branches had fallen on the fence wires. Occasionally a fence post would have to be, replaced. My part of this job as a lad was to go down the fence line, find all the broken fence posts. I could pull the post out of line so Dad could spot it.

One sunny afternoon as I was checking posts, I noticed some puppies playing by the old black walnut tree. I was playing with them and watching them chase a stick. Then I heard Dad tell me to get out of there. They were not puppies but real young fox! I thought that they were cute! I had fun till Dad showed up.

I also helped string new barbed wire where there was a need for it. I carried staples, the hammer and the fence pliers. When I got older I already knew how to put the hook of the pliers in by the staple and use the hammer to drive out the old staple. I would pull the wire on the far side of the fence post and push the wire to the post with my knee. Next, I would pound the new staple into the post with the hammer to securing the wire tight. I could only help with the fence after school and on Saturdays. It was the same with the plowing and dragging. Dad had a two-horse plow with a seat. The drag was much bigger. You still stood on the back bar, or you walked at the side.

The plow and the drag were bigger so Dad could get more work done in less time.

Once it was warmer, and the fence was fixed, we let the cows out during the day. After school, Mom had a new job for Jessie and me. The wild strawberries grew along the banks towards the creek and over on the Ellsworth road next to our property, so we picked wild strawberries until chore time. They sure were good on warm biscuits with fresh home made whipped cream. Homemade whipped cream, made right from our own cream, from off the top of the cans of milk. There were also currants; black berries; elderberries; and raspberries. They were all good! I remember that after chores in August we could always go up near the woods and pick blackberries. We would use the milk pails and fill them in no time at all. There were plenty of them. Mom always put up about eighty quarts a year. The currents grew right next to the dirt road we lived on. Mom made many jars of current jam each year as well. Over near the milk house, usually in August or September, the elderberry bush was loaded and mom made elderberry jam, pies, and canned some for the winter. I think one of the hardest jobs was picking the wild strawberries in June. They were very tiny but very sweet.

School was out now and summer had begun. With summer, came hay season. We cut the hay the same way I mentioned in one of the previous chapters. When I got older, I had more responsibility. I found myself on a dump rake raking hay one afternoon. It was fun but that old steel handle had to be pulled each time you came to the row of hay and it gave me some really sore blisters. Dad had forgotten to give me gloves!

After chores the next day, Dad went out to the field to check the hay. When he came back, I helped him harness up the horses and we went out back to hitch up to the hay wagon. Someone had brought a hay wagon to us from the auction house. It was a flat wagon with high sides on it. There was a front that went up as high as the sides and fastened to them. Dad backed the wagon up to the hay loader, and hooked it on to the frame of the wagon. We went up to the field where the horses and wagon straddled the row of hay. I had to get up on the high cross over piece on the front of the wagon. Dad threw the lines for the horses up to me and then went to the back of the wagon, with a pitchfork and pulled the lever on the hay loader. He told me to drive the horses.

As we went forward, and the hay loader, with all its hooks, drew the hay up and over the back of the wagon. Dad used the pitchfork to distribute the hay around the wagon, and I had to make sure the horses did not go too fast. If they did, it could bury my Dad with the hay! Usually, by the time I got to the other end of the field, the wagon was full. At this point, I had the horses stopped, and Dad would unhook the hay loader. He climbed on the whipple trees behind the horses, and I drove them back to the barn. At the barn, Dad took Dan by the bridle and would lead both horses and wagon up into the barn, staying as close as they could to the left side of the haymow. This left room for him to unhook Molly and back her out of the barn. My job was to hook Molly up to the trip rope. Dad got up into the wagon and released the haymow fork that was up in the peek of the barn. It was a large fork and had two hooks one on each side of it. Dad would take his feet and stomp on this fork getting it down into as much hay as he could. I would then lead Molly forward, pulling the rope, which pulled up the fork load of hay until it plugged into the roller, in the rail at the top of the barn ceiling. As soon as I heard it plug in I stopped Molly and the fork of hay would go across the top of the mow until Dad tripped it by the small rope attached. The hay dropped on the mow and the fork would return to Dad. This was repeated until the wagon was unloaded, and Dad brought Molly back inside the barn and hooked her up, and then backed the team and wagon out. We got a drink, usually Kool-Aid or Royal Crown soda. On occasion Mom would make homemade root beer or home made switchel, which was a nice drink in the hot summer. After we finished our drink, we headed back to the field again. As you can tell, haying was much different back then.

I do not recall much else about the place up in the hollow. My wife and I drove by there a few years ago and there was nothing left. There is, however, a brand new home there now and everything looks so different.

The next part of my life was another chapter entirely. We would be moving again! Dad wanted to quit share cropping and just become a hired man on a farm. But this farm would be quite different for us. They had tractors and were a bit more modern. A lot of changes are in store for us.

4

FROM HORSES TO TRACTORS

We moved from the Unadilla Valley over to Preston Hill, about twenty miles to the west. It is located five miles from Earlville, New York, five miles from Hamilton, New York, and about three miles from Poolville, New York. Preston Hill is rural farm country. Dad went to work for "Pappy" Miller. Pappy had two sons, Alfred and Don, who also had farms right next door. These three farms were known as the Miller Farms. Pappy and his wife had a big duplex house, and we moved in on one side of the duplex. It was a lot nicer than the houses we had lived in. This house had a wood furnace that warmed the water and forced the water through the pipes so that each room had a hot water register. WOW! Heat in each room! This was living in luxury! The house located about two tenths of a mile from the barn which made for an easy walking distance. Pappy usually took the flatbed truck, as this was the truck used for many different jobs around the farm. Including, hauling the milk from all three farms to the creamery. The truck was Ford, almost new! My job was to get the cows to and from the pasture in the summer months. I also helped with the feeding of the cows; and giving milk to the newborn calves. The milk for the calves was usually milk from a cow that had just freshened (had a calf) and the milk could not be sent to the creamery for about four to five days. I also helped clean the barn before I ate my breakfast. It was much easier to clean the gutters now with a barn cleaner. No more shoveling! Then, on Saturdays, I helped get wood for the wood furnace and swept cobwebs in the barn on rainy days. The barn had to be as clean as possible in case a milk inspector came by. If the inspector found it in a dirty condition, he may perhaps stop your milk from being accepted at the creamery. If that happened, the milk check would be much smaller for that month.

It sure was different being around tractors. The different types of tractors were: a Ferguson thirty; a McCormick F-thirty; a Farmall-H; a Farmall-M; and a Farmall "Super" M. All of these tractors were used where needed on all three farms. I was allowed to use the Ferguson Thirty to drive around from farm to farm!

One of the big differences for us was that Pappy Miller drove a 1961, Mercury. He actually gave my dad the old Hudson that sat up in the back yard. The fuel pump did not work. What happened was you went as fast as you could when you came to a hill. When the car would begin to sputter dad would coast it back, around facing back down the hill. This allowed the gas to flow toward the engine and run. Then, we would proceed to back up the hill to the top. He then turned it around and we kept on going! Alfred Miller had the brand new Mercury, while Don Miller had a '48 Ford coupe. To me they were all nice cars.

The school I attended my first year there was in Poolville, New York. It was the grade school and branch of the Earlville school system. I only had one year there before I went to Earlville for Jr. High. Poolville was a small school with no sports due to the fact there was no space for a ball field. It consisted of two large rooms where grades Kindergarten through sixth grade were. So, for a sixth grader, I was glad I could get a workout at the farm.

Since we now had a car for our family of five, we started going to church in North Brookfield. This is where many of my parents' friends went. This is also where my Aunt Doris went to church. She was the one who gave me my first children's story Bible. There was a woman in this church that had been friends with my parents for years from Waterville, New York. Her name was Alice King. It was either Alice, or her sister, that had a crush on Dad before he married my mom. Alice drove all the way over to Earlville and picked up my sister, Jessie, and me for Sunday school and youth meetings. Then my parents would come later to church after the chores. Usually, after church on Sunday, we had sandwiches and a drink in the car for a picnic on the way home. Occasionally, Aunt Doris and Uncle Cliff would invite us to their house just down around the corner from the church for dinner. Three or four times a year we would go up the railroad tracks to Mom's parents, Grandpa and Grandma Clemens. Most of the summer on Sundays, we would have our picnic over on the corner of Carl's Inn in Madison, New York. That is where Julius Waterman had a camper trailer set up, with another trailer that held two Buffalo. My Grandpa Pierce and Mr. Waterman had trained these two buffalo from calves. Many of the county and state fairs had horse pulls and after the horses had finished pulling Grandpa and Mr. Waterman would enter the two buffalo and show how they could also pull as a team. Another thing they would use them for is plowing fields for farmers in the area. This gave them a little extra money or food. Sundays, we would stop by there often, and I would feed them hay and give them water. Then Mr. Waterman gave me a ride on one of them. It was a lot of fun. My mom had pictures of me on them, but I do not know what ever happened to those pictures. A few years later Mr. Waterman became the local barber.

Getting back to Alice King, she would come over to the farm and take me to youth meetings that were held at that time in Mrs. Carol Head's house. Carol Head was the church pianist, and did many other jobs for the church. It was at one of these youth meetings that I began to notice a pretty, little girl there. She had a bunch of brothers (four to be exact) and two sisters. She sure was pretty! I found out that her name was Patricia Stone. They called her Patti. Youth meetings were fun. I hoped that she had not noticed me looking at her occasionally. After the meeting and some snacks, Alice King took me back home. On the way home I asked her about Patti. She told me that she was from Kelly Stone family. WOW! I had heard my mom and dad talk of them. They were farm folk over in Madison, real respectable people!

Boy, I needed to be ever so careful.

I remember Christmas that year was different for us. We not only had an orange and a coloring book, in our stockings, there was store candy and a piece of bubble gum. Then, we received a box of candy and an orange at church that year. This sure was nice of everybody! We spent Christmas with Grandma & Grandpa Clemens, on two different years, Aunt Doris & Uncle Cliff were there and Mom's brother, Uncle Ernie. I remember Uncle Ernie because he worked on the Arthur Welch farm painting the barns. I found out that after we left the Welch farm, uncle Ernie was planning to marry Arthur Welch's oldest daughter, Elrina. They planned to go to Bible College. Anyhow, he brought a giant kettle of spaghetti! At least once in the afternoon the train would go down past our grandparent's house and we thought that it was really something exciting! It was a lot bigger train than the steam engine over in Unadilla Valley! About four o'clock in the afternoon, we all headed back home to do the barn chores.

Winter seemed to go by quickly between chores, wood, and maple sugar time. One of the big events that winter was that Don Miller's barn burned. Without a barn, his cows were put in with the other two herds. This brought some new activity. Pappy, Don, and Alfred spent day after day in the woods cutting logs for a new barn in the spring. As much as I could, I helped in the woods. Alfred had a Mall two-man chain saw. I helped hold and push the smaller end of that saw through many trees. I was now officially involved in logging, cutting off branches with an axe and helping hook up the chain for the hauling of the logs with the tractor. I guess it's called "branching out". I was learning that there was a lot involved with farming.

Spring was coming and Pappy left much of the farm chores to Dad and me. He spent a lot of time down at Alfred's place. That was where the saw-mill was. He was cutting beams and lumber for the new barn to be built, at Don Miller's, as soon as the weather broke nice enough. It was fun to help roll the logs' when I had time. We used thick long-handle poles with a point on the end and a swing-hook. We poked into the log and the swing hook caught the bark of the log. When this happened we pulled toward us, and the log rolled down onto the trough. This trough had slats on it that brought the logs up to the big saw. Pappy then measured and adjusted the thickness of the cut that he wanted to make. The first step was cutting the four sides off, removing the bark and some of the wood, which later would be sawn into small pieces. This became slab wood for the wood stoves. This left nice pieces to work with and he began to measure and cut the thick main beams for the barn. He also cut two-inch thick pieces needed for lumber siding. Some were six inches, or four inches, whatever he thought he would need. The beams that he cut were then placed on the trough and measured for the proper width of the lumber that he felt that he needed. As it cut away the edge it left these nice pieces of lumber which were stacked in a pile. The edgings were smaller than the slabs above and were sawn and made into firewood.. Now, I am telling you this because there were no, Home Depots, or Lowe's back in those days. You cut your own lumber, or you knew some one else that had a lumber mill that would cut your lumber for you.

Pappy had already measured and marked off the length and the width of the barn with red flags. As soon as the ground would thaw, he would start the process of the foundation. This was going to be something big to watch, and maybe even get involved in! A barn rising happened that spring and through the summer! Many local farmers came to help. It turned out to be a big barn!

As soon as the weather was warmer and the ground was not frozen, it was once again fence-mending time. All of my free time off from school would be fence mending. I helped on all three farms in this matter. They all wanted to get the cows out to pasture as soon as possible so they could work on the forms for the foundation of the new barn. However, there was also the plowing, disking, dragging, and preparation of getting the oats in by the middle of May. Things really got busy! When we were finished with the fences, I helped pick stones out of the field; and I did my first tractor work of cleaning barns, spreading manure, dragging and having a good time! The last crop to get into the ground was the corn. It was usually in the ground by Memorial Day.

Sometimes it was the first week of June. We would strive for Memorial Day giving us a day off to go to town to see the parade! A day off was always a blessing!

By now, you realize that farm work is never finished. There is always something to do. Even on rainy days, there are pieces of equipment to fix, cows to feed and to milk, clean and sweep cobwebs in the barn so that it was ready to white wash. There was also the heifer barn to clean out as well. There was never, never a dull day!

The Barn building is also in full swing!! Let us see in the next chapter what God has in store!

5

A BARN RISING

I will try to tell you all that I learned and a lot that I cannot remember all regarding the building of the new barn "Etc." The first thing was the digging of the foundation by a contractor with a backhoe. Next, wooden forms were nailed together and these were to be used for the foundation. (This is what the cement would be poured into). The trucks arrived and dumped stone, gravel, and sand, which would be mixed with the cement mixer and poured into the forms. After each section of the cement was poured, and before the cement hardened fully, we placed large long bolts into the soft cement at certain intervals. The threads of the bolts stuck up out of the cement so many inches apart. Pappy Miller already had planks cut with holes that corresponded to the distance of each bolt. Pappy would lay the planks of lumber on the cement, with the bolts coming up out of them. As the cement hardened I went around and placed large washers on the bolts with the nuts started. The next step was to tighten the nuts with a wrench. The pieces of siding were then placed upright and then nailed to the plank at the bottom and the support beam at the top. Also, there were large support beams; hardened in the cement on each corner and at certain intervals along the sides of the barn.

Once all of that had fully hardened, the next step was to raise the large beams up on the support beams that stuck upward. These were long beams going the full length of the barn. If I remember correctly, there were six of these along each side and two on both ends of the barn. These were the carrier beams because they would be carrying the weight of the roof. At each of the sections, where they joined the upright beams, a notch was cut just enough for the beam to sit on the upright. Then a two or three-inch hole was tapped out. Wooden pegs were driven through the holes and fastened the beam secure. To make it even more secure, pieces of two by-six boards were slant-cut on each end, and put up on angle between the upright beam and the carrier beam at each one of the uprights, including the corner.

Before the barn was completed, it was time for haying season to begin. The farm work had to continue. School was going to be out in one week for summer break! Praise the Lord! Oh, how I liked to be part of all that was happening on each of the farms! Pappy Miller spent all his time now at the site of the new barn. The main barn floor was completed and the cement hardened. It looked very nice! Pappy began to put siding on the outside of the first floor of the barn. He had the lumber cut for the upstairs floor, which of course would become the hay floor of the barn. Don and Alfred helped when they could, but the haying had to get started. The haying, or any field work, and the gathering of the crops always started at one farm and went to the next until it was finished at all three farms, only to start all over again with second cutting.

Finally, I was out of school for the summer! After I ate my lunch that day, I went with Dad down to Don Miller's place where they had just started to bale the hay for the summer. The hay was going to go to the heifer barn this time since the new barn was not completed. Don was up in the field baling hay and Alfred, Dad, and I went up to the field with the tractor and hay wagon. Back then one person drove the tractor, another man stacked the hay on the wagon (usually me), and another one or two men would go along on the ground and throw the bales onto the wagon. There was kind of an art to loading the wagon. We started by crisscrossing the end bales on each level, so that the load stayed together while going down the side hill. Not only did we have a side hill to go down from this particular field, it was part of the cow pasture and rough. We finally finished loading the wagon, and Dad and Alfred were on the tractor, while I was up on top of the load. Since I stacked the load, this is where I ended up. We approached the downhill and we went slowly because it was a side hill. About half way down the front tire on the wagon blew. It was on the down-hill-side and I can still remember slowly falling off the top of that load of hay. Unfortunately, I landed on my right hand that hit a stone, and I hit the stone with all my weight. Alfred stopped the tractor and came to help me up. I got up and thought that I was o.k. We re-loaded the hay and headed on down to the barn with the flat. By the time we reached the barn with part of the load of hay and a flat tire, I began to notice that the leather band on my watch was very tight on my right wrist. You guessed it, my wrist was really swollen and hurting. Alfred took me to Earlville, New York to the doctor's office where a cast was put on my wrist and some pain medicine given. The thing I remember most was the fact that I did not get my "cold" Royal Crown soda drink that day! This was always a treat after each load of hay. Oh man! Summer, had just started for me... and look at the shape I was in! I would not be much help around the farm that summer. However, I did drive tractor a lot: racking hay, pulling the hay wagons, and cultivating the corn. I also dragged boards for Pappy down at the new barn as he put siding on, and as he paved the barn floor with cement. It seemed that summer went by too slowly.

Finally, the haying was finished and as usual, Pappy came out to us with some half gallons of ice cream! He took a knife and cut the boxes into 4 pieces. We each got a quarter of a box to eat. He said that it was tradition. I immediately thought it was a real nice tradition! WOW! Ice cream was a real treat.

Alfred helped me cut the cast off my wrist the Saturday before Labor Day. He always hired a man to do chores on Labor Day, and took me, with his family, to the New York State fair! It was sure exciting for me! The exhibits, square-dance music, while new super C Farmall tractors were doing the square dancing! It was fun to watch. I could hardly believe it! They bought me a sausage and pepper sandwich. I never had anything like that before. It was grreeaaat! At night, before we left the fairgrounds, there were fire works. I had never seen these before either! WOW! I even spent some of my allowance, which was $20.00 a week at that time. I won a Teddy bear for my mom. I seemed to have a bit of luck making my nickel land on a glass plate. (I have forgotten how many times I had to do this to win the teddy bear though). I believe that it was only four or five times.

After Labor Day, came the first day school! I was in seventh grade, that year. So much to do on the farm, and here I was stuck at school. Dad told me he only finished sixth grade and wanted me to graduate. The worse part of going back to school was the fact that the men were right in the middle of corn harvest time. I loved this time of year, with the smell of fresh chopped corn! Back in those days Alfred did the chopping while someone drove along side the chopper with a corn wagon. These wagons were equipped with an apron chain like the manure spreader. As the wagon drove side the corn chopper, it would eventually get full. Then, as that person brought it to the silo, another person with a wagon would take their place beside the chopper. The person heading to the silo blower would back up to the blower and hook on the drive shaft, which would go into the apron on the wagon floor. There was a tractor with a pulley and belt, which turned the drive shaft, and pulled the apron chain and corn toward the back of the wagon. One or two people would be there with the hook forks pulling the corn down and trying to keep it even in the blower trough. This trough also had an apron chain, which carried the corn to the large hole at the end and into the blower wheel. The pulley turned the blower wheel fast, and as the corn hit the wheel, it would go up the blower pipe and into the silo. If there happened to be too much corn on the blower it would plug the blower and pipe, then everything stopped. Pipes had to be taken apart, and all had to be unplugged. My job was feeding the corn into the blower. When the silo was almost half full, someone had to be in the silo distributing the corn around evenly and stomping it down as hard as you could get it. This kept a lot of air out of the corn, and kept it from rotting. I liked the silo filling days and always looked forward to coming home from school and helping. Little did I know that God was going to use silo filling to change our lives in a drastic way!

God is at work in the lives of his children! God never moves without purpose or plan.

6

A HEART WRENCHING EXPERIENCE!

One particular day, as I came home from school, I thought about how I would be helping with at least one or two loads of corn. However, as the school bus drove by Don Miller's farm, I noticed, up on the side hill a tractor and wagon that had overturned, and no one was around. I thought that it was odd. When I got off the school bus, I noticed Don's new pick-up was there, and Alfred's car. Something was… really, strange! When I went in the house, Don told me that there had been an accident involving my dad and the tractor. Pappy and Mrs. Miller had taken my mom down to Hamilton hospital. My dad was in very bad shape. Alfred took me by the hand and led me to his car to take me to the hospital to see my dad. I was numb! I could not cry, I really did not want to go, but I knew that I should. When we arrived, we waited in the emergency room for a long time. No one spoke a word. Alfred and Pappy had to leave to go and do chores while Pappy's wife stayed with us. It was late when they took us back to a room so we could see Dad. Mom went in the room with my sister Jessie for a few minutes and then Jessie came out while I went in. I can still to this day, tell you exactly what I saw. He had a blanket that covered him up to his shoulders. Above his shoulders was one thick bandage. All you could see was one eye, all the tubes, and he could not talk. The nurse told us he could hear and understand some, but she did not know how much because of the heavy medicine. Days and weeks went by until we finally heard that he could talk. It was after the sixth week. One of the things you need to understand is that my Dad was a heavy smoker. He smoked at least a pack of Camel cigarettes a day. One of the nurses told us that when he first was able to talk he asked her for a cigarette. She told him, "No!" Then he asked her how long he had been there, and she told him it was six weeks. My dad said that if he had been there six weeks and did not have a cigarette then he did not need one now! From that day, and for the rest of his life, he never smoked.

I was busy with school and helping on the farm at Pappy's, where dad worked trying to do as much of Dad's work as I possibly could. It was better to be busy. I later learned what had happened the day of Dad's accident. While chopping corn on a side hill, one of the things that you need to do is keep the chopper tractor and the wagon tractor moving. As long as you are moving forward, the tractors are not so prone to tip-over. They had worked half way up the side hill with no trouble. That particular time while they were going along the chopper for some reason had plugged. The natural reaction was to stop, which everybody did. Alfred was unplugging the chopper and Dad was just sitting there waiting. Alfred happened to look over to Dad and saw that the rear tire of the tractor that dad was on was off the ground! Dad, at the same time, also realized the tractor was going to tip over. My dad was six foot three inches tall and had a thirteen-and-a-half size shoe. His right shoe was on the brake of the tractor while stopped. As the tractor was going over, he tried to jump clear but his foot caught in the brake pedals. These tractors had both brake pedals on the right side. As Dad's foot caught, he could not get clear of the tractor, and as the tractor went over it pinned him to the ground with the fender. The right side of his face and jaw plus part of his upper torso was pinned. Alfred told me that there was an actual indent made in the ground.

I was only thirteen years old and with Dad in the hospital mom did not have an income. She did get a few groceries from the Millers. I had been trying to sort this out. In a young boy's head, it was not easy. Alfred came to me one day after school and asked me if I would come and board with his family and he would give me $20 a week. He told me that, if I wanted to, I could give Mom some and help her out. So, I said, "Yes!" If they wanted to put up with this old farm boy, I was willing! That is how I came to leave home at the age of thirteen, and started boarding on the Alfred Miller farm.

It was also at this time that Mom had someone from the North Brookfield church coming to help her. Her name was "Grandma" Austin to all of us. I especially remember the day that she came. The car pulled up and to my surprise, was that pretty, little girl from the youth meetings, Patti! I met her parents Kelly and Flossy Stone and Grandma Austin. After a few minutes, I asked if Patti could go with me on the tractor. It had a little wood box on the back, so Patti sat on it as I drove around. We stopped and talked just a bit before we went back home. I was so excited that I didn't know what to do! At least we knew each other existed! Youth meetings and church were a bit more interesting now! Her Grandma Austin stayed about three weeks helping mom with dad after he came home.

I was a hired man now, so I helped all I could at Alfred's farm and also, at the new barn with Pappy. It was coming along fine. It was almost ready for the rafters to go up in place. We all got together for a few days and did this. As the men, pulled the rafters up in place, my job was to drive a nail in both sides of the foot of the rafter to hold it. Once a few of the rafters were up, Pappy showed me how to go up the ladder with roof boards. We would nail the roof boards to the rafters every few feet up to the peek. It sure was high up there, but I never really was afraid of heights. Some men worked on the rafters while others did the roof boards. When we were finally done, a big truck came with all the tin roofing. The men put the roofing on while I was in school. It only took them two days. That is all I remember of the barn raising and the summer and fall that went by so quickly. There were good times and the sad times, with Dad's accident. I realize that each farmer has similar tales to tell if prompted to do so.

I am glad for all the experiences and the lessons learned through them. I realized that God was teaching me these lessons for future reference. God never moves without purpose or plan. In the process He molds the person to be exactly what He wants him or her to be if that person is willing.

Because of dad's accident, and his limitations, he could not do the work on the Miller farms that they wanted him to do. This meant that we will be moving again. Therefore, another chapter is about to start.

7

LEARNING... ABOUT MISSIONS!

Our family now moved back to the Unadilla valley. Dad had a job back on the Arthur Welch farm, the farm that sits just south of where we first lived on route #8. I have many fond memories of this place. It was here that some new beginnings happened in my life.

This farm had an apple orchard which was by the cow pasture it also had a building that was a chicken house on one end, and a pigpen on the other end. Not only did we have most of the same kinds of wild fruit, there were lots of, wild grapes that grew along the fence by the house. The garden area was quite large. That kept all of us busy in the summer. The barn was down across the road from the house. The road, route 8 seemed to be a bit busier than I had remembered it.

Dad had his car, a 1950 Chevy; there was a 1956 Chevy pick-up on the farm. Also, there was a team of horses, and thirty cows. Back then it was a moderate size farm. After Mr. Arthur Welch sold the farm up in the hollow, he had bought this one, which was only a quarter mile from the main farm where he lived.

One of the new beginnings was the tug of Missions on my heart. I did not realize it for a few years. Next door to us was the little house that we first lived in before moving up to the Hollow. I met the young man and his new wife that lived there, Chick and Joan Watkins. They took me to church one Sunday when Dad was sick. He told me that they were going to Africa to be missionaries. Wow! I never had a friend like that before! He was learning how to fly. I remember the day when Dad and I were out in the field and I heard an airplane.

It circled around the field a couple of times, and was low to the ground! All at once it came over our apple trees and landed in the hay field that went from our place to Arthur's place. You have to realize that it was about a quarter of a mile between the two farms, and this one particular hay lot was accessible from both farms. The hay had been recently harvested.

Dad did not talk much about things; he was a quiet man. However, he did say, "That's strange". We headed to the barn for chores and we heard the plane as it went over our house and apple orchard again. It was after chores and supper was finished that Dad went up to the main farm to see Mr. Welch. When he came back, he told us that Chick would be practicing landing on the field quite a lot, as he needed to practice for the small airfields in Africa.

It was on one of these days of practice that we all were up on the main farm; Dad and I, with Arthur and his two boys, Clayton and Charlie. Chick landed and opened his door and asked if anybody wanted to ride. WOW! We took turns one at a time going up with him in the plane. It was bumpy going across the hayfield. However, we surely enjoyed the rides; and Chick had a lot of practice that day.

Chick & Joan sang together with the guitar, Chick also did a few solos. I used to go to their house in the evenings some times. I had an old harmonica that my uncle Ernie gave me and he would find the right key and we played together. We finally had a couple of songs where we did a good job! He and Joan went to quite a few churches in the area and church groups explaining the purpose of their mission endeavors, Later, I realized that what they were doing was called deputation. One night after we practiced he asked if I wanted to go with them to North Brookfield, N.Y. (remember, I knew a sweet girl in the teen group over there by the name of Patti Stone.) Chick informed me that we would be going to the farm of Frank & Bernie Key. Many of the church folk from N. Brookfield Baptist church would be there for a picnic. My answer, of course, was I would like to go with them. The farm was next to right 12 in N. Brookfield, just west of the church. I am here to tell you they had a "spread!" At least four picnic tables, all lined up with food! I was a bit nervous, as I had never played my harmonica in public, PLUS, Patti's parents were there! Her aunt and uncle, Raymond & Mildred Stone, were also there. Her Aunt Carol, where we used to go and have youth meetings, was there also. This was a bit much for this young boy! After the meal, we had our time of songs, and Chick & Joan shared the work that they would be doing in Africa. It was indeed a fun night!

I must share here that I also experienced something new for me a few months later. Joan was going to have a baby. We had just arrived home from Church (our home church), and Joan was very uncomfortable. I did not understand many of the issues regarding this at the time. Chick went into the bathroom with her. When he came out he was shouting, "Were going to have a baby! Let's go!" We went to the hospital, which was in New Berlin, New York. I do not remember how long it was, but Chick came and told me that they had a son, Nathan! Then we came back to his house and had pizza. He was naturally quite excited.

Chick would have Nathan on his lap trying to drive the car at 3 months old. I am not sure if Nathan ever knew that he started driving his dads old Nash Rambler. Of course he had his dads help!

One afternoon, Dad told me that we were going up to Arthur's, to help that afternoon. When we arrived, we noticed some plywood and two-by-fours. Also there were steel barrels there. A few of the men from the church had come to make crates for some of Chick & Joan's household goods. They were putting many things in barrels. Yep! They were packing up and getting everything ready to ship their things overseas! (I never in a million years thought that I would be doing this in a few years.)

Dear reader, if you recall I used to be a boarder, back on the Alfred Miller farm. Now I had the opportunity to do it again on a different farm. The Leo Johnson farm right next door to Mom and Dad wanted me to come. I took the job! Leo and his wife, Theresa were a real nice couple. They had a little boy named Timmy. It seemed that I not only was to help on the farm but also help take care of Timmy, their son. Three times that summer; they would have me take Timmy; the tent; some sandwiches and juice, up by the pond where we would camp out overnight. One of the other fun things was driving their '57 Ford pick-up around, doing farm jobs such as hauling sawdust, hay and other things. They also had a '57 Dodge car that I had the privilege to drive twice, once from the Dye farm where Leo rented land; and the other time when I took Theresa to a dance at school. Leo would not take her and she really wanted to go. She had me take her.

My sister, Jessie, was a good friend of Patti Stone back when we lived in Earlville, New York and attended North Brookfield church. Apparently, she noticed that I was not interested in the girls there in New Berlin where we were going now. One night when I went home to visit Mom and Dad, Jessie said she was going to invite Patti over for a weekend. I thought that to be very interesting! The weekend, I went home after my chores to visit. Then on Sunday after church, my mom and dad were taking Patti back to her house. Dad mentioned that it was too bad I could not ride along. I went over to the farm and asked Leo if I could go with my parents. He said that I could. Dad had a '52 Willie's wagon and plenty of room, so I went. At the Stone farm, while the parents were talking, I went out and sat at the picnic table on the front lawn. Before long, out came Patti and she sat on the other side. I do not even know if we talked. All I remember is that when Jessie and my parents came out to leave, Patti asked me if I would write her, I told her, "yes!" When I got back to the farm, Leo was watching television with Timmy. Teresa came to the kitchen and asked me how it went. I tried not to say anything, but she knew something was up. I told her Patti wanted me to write her. She immediately got me paper and pen-cil, and proceeded to tell me what to write. Then she sealed it and sent it on its way.

By the time I was seventeen, I had taken my drivers license on Clare Maxin's brand new '58 Chevy. Their son Larry and I spent many

Sunday afternoons together when we were young. I also had worked there, at Johnson's long enough to have just a little money saved up. I went with dad one day over to Earlville, New York to see Mr. Silas Baker to buy my first car! Mr. Baker had the Chevy dealership there in town, and he had a big interest in the local bank. Dad had bought a couple cars from him and I was interested in what I could find. Mr. Baker then showed me a few cars and took me over to a '51 Plymouth, Cranberry, 4-door. It was in good shape. We tried it out, but I told him that it had a little noise in the motor. He told me the car was fine and that he would stand behind what he sold. I bought it for $500 dollars and drove it home. Then Dad took the dealer plate back. It was another 5 months before I had the money for the insurance, and I went up to Leonardsville, New York and got my insurance from an agent there that Leo used. What a Saturday night this was going to be! After chores I picked up my sister Jessie and we then headed to New Berlin to a youth meeting. The only problem was that the noise in the motor got much louder. You guessed it! The motor seized up! Some people stopped and picked us up and took us the rest of the way to the meeting. After the meeting, we rode home with Clayton Welch who had his dad's '55 Chevy. Monday morning, Leo called Mr. Baker and told him about the Plymouth. Much to my surprise, he came to where the car was, just north of New Berlin and towed the car back to his shop and three weeks later he called and asked us to come and get the car. He had a '48 out back that had been rear-ended. He took the motor out of it and put it in my car. He never charged me a dime! WOW! Can you believe it? A $500 car and he changed the motor and made it right!

Now my story becomes more interesting! When I did not have my car, Leo used to let me have the pick-up and go see Patti. Then, when I had my own car, I really liked going over to North Brookfield Baptist Church and worship with her.

One Sunday while I was there in North Brookfield, Mrs. Clyde Head (Millie), asked me if I would be interested in boarding with them and helping them out. This way I would be much closer to the church the church. It also would put me much closer to where Patti lived. I really liked the Johnson's where I was, but to be closer to Patti...oh boy!

Another chapter is about to unfold!

8

THE NINE MILE SWAMP

I arrived at the Clyde Head farm, with Clyde; Millie; and their two sons, Dewitt and Richie. The farm is located on the west side of the Nine Mile Swamp! I had heard some stories about this area from my grandfather when he lived "up the swamp." They say that the famous "Loomis Gang" was responsible for stealing cows and horses from local farmers and selling them. (This can be documented in any public Library or internet.) I was on a farm just down the road from where they had their underground cave, which was the hiding place for stolen animals.

One of the things I learned real fast was that Clyde Head was a brother to Patti's Uncle Cart Head who was married to Aunt Carol where I used to go for youth meetings. Then up the road, one half, mile was Junior Head. He also was a brother to Clyde. The three brothers not only had the three farms, but they all worked together. For example: if it was haying season, we would all go to one farm and do the haying, then on to the next, and then the last farm.

One thing I really enjoyed about these Head Brothers. The fact that if one of them had a birthday, then after morning chores were done that day, we would go to that brother's house and play table games, softball, or just talk, maybe sing some choruses. Then when it was time for lunch we would have a big meal. To me this was fun!

I also need to tell those of you who are wondering, that yes, they all had tractors. I had my '51 Plymouth, and enjoyed the farm with tractors! It was a dream coming true! Here at Clyde & Millie Head's, we had newer tractors than I had been able to be around before. One was a Farmall H, and the other was an Oliver 88. Both of these tractors were quite a tractor back then in 1959. They also had a little Ford 30 that we used for doing odd jobs, such as mending fences, etc. They all were fun to work since I came from the old horse days originally.

My job actually, was getting up at 4:30 a.m. for chores and getting the milking machines and pails all out on the barn floor. I would get the silage or hay down for the cows, then clean behind them, and feed "old Dan." Dan, was a two-ton bull that we used for breeding, he was a purebred bull. All three farms had purebred cows. Then I would take the old '49 Dodge and go up to the heifer barn. I fed the heifers their silage or hay, and then cleaned the barn and spread the manure. By the time I finished all of these chores, it was time to get back to the house, wash up, change my clothes and go to school.

Once a month a milk tester would come and take a sample of each, cow's milk, (both night, and morning). That meant he would spend the night with us in order to be there in the morning. These samples were taken and tested for butterfat content. Then he would weigh the milk for each cow, night and morning to get a record of the amount of milk each cow produced. All this information gave us the fat level, of the milk, (the higher the better) and total production of each cow for the official Holstein records. The fat level usually was about three to four points, which was good. It also gave us an average pound weight, for milk for each cow. I remember that we had some that would produce very well. We had five that used to top the chart for the purebred association. This was evident in the fact that we had people from way out west that waned to buy heifer calves from these cows if we had any we wanted to sell. However, most of them were kept as replacements. With purebred cows, each calf that was born had to have a drawing on record. Someone had to look at the calf from each side and draw on the paper the variations of the black and white. You now realize that black and white means that they were Holsteins.

The following are some of the jobs that I did around the farm. I helped mend fence, pick stones out of the field, clean the barn, I spread manure, put the milking machines together, clean the mangers, throw the hay down from the hay mow, putt the silage down, and other small jobs like sweeping cobwebs "etc.". In the haying season, I loaded the hay wagons, or did the racking of the hay for the baler. When the haying was finished, it meant that I would take the scythe and cut down burdocks and grass around the barn and milk house. I helped in disking & dragging preparing the fields for planting the crops. Around the farm there was always enough to keep you busy.

My old Plymouth finally wore out and I bought a '52 Ford that had a '56 Olds engine in it, which meant it was a constant tinker toy. We had to change the starting system from a generator system to an alternator system. This was because cars changed from generators to alternators in 1955. It was quite a challenge but we did get it working by using from separate starter solenoid. However, as soon as the engine started you had to shut this extra solenoid off immediately. The car was a "tinker toy" and always had to be worked on, so, I traded it in for a '53 Cadillac. I was a senior in High School with a Cadillac…(not bad)!

I also tried my artistic skills and did some barn painting. The barn was badly in need of paint and Clyde wanted me to help paint it. The high sides, plus the ends of the barn did not bother me. I was not afraid of heights, even climbing the silos. Now, I must let you know that the barn was built, very close to the road. It also was on a rather sharp corner just about like a "T." The road came by the front of the barn and turned right up past the West Side of the barn. The one thing that got my attention, one day, was a particular new 1958 Ford "blue station wagon" that kept going back and forth, not far from my ladder! It got my attention because it was Patti, learning to drive her daddy's stick-shift wagon. She sure was a cutie!

Another thing that I liked here on the farm was the dog that Clyde had. Many of the farms in the area had the same breed of dog and all of them, had been trained to herd the cows. When the cows were out to pasture in the summer time, we just had the dog jump in the back of the truck and go to the pasture gate. Once there we opened the gate and the dog would go round up the cows and bring them down the road, into the barnyard and into the barn. He then waited till we were done milking, usually about two and a half hours. Then, when we let the cows loose, he would take them out of the barnyard, up the road, and into the pasture. Then he would sit there and wait until we came and closed the gate. What a dog! He was a real good woodchuck hunter as well. Sometimes, after the morning chores were finished, and we were eating breakfast, Dewitt, the older son, would get the dog roused up and it would take little Richie's pants cuff and drag him around the linoleum kitchen floor. Richie did not like it too well, but the dog enjoyed it! It sure was a nice farm.

One night, after I went out on a date with Patti, as I came back to the farm, I came over the knoll and I realized that there were no lights on anywhere at the farm. Clyde sat on a chair by the table with his head in his hands. I asked him what was going on, and all he could do was point to the barn. I went out toward the barn and discovered that the silo had fallen over; crushed the milk house, and knocked out the transformer for the electric. WOW! Patti's Uncle Raymond and I had been up in that silo just that afternoon. We were stomping silage trying to get as much as we could into it. I remember that we heard popping noises at different times all afternoon. It was a metal silo and the rivets were coming apart. GOD had watched over us and kept us safe!! Praise His name! Cart and Junior Head each took a part of the cows to milk. We gave them our milking machines and equipment. We spent most of our time cleaning up debris and getting set for the building of a new silo. I must say that I did miss a lot of school that late fall and early winter. I was out of school for 30 days.

The main activity, out side the farm was Church and School. It was a lot of fun at church! Young people's meeting where I could see Patti, we sang in the choir, we also played in the orchestra. I played trumpet, and she played violin. There were also many church luncheons, or suppers, and teen meetings.

One thing that I remember was that Pastor Slater enjoyed going to a supper once a month with just the men. It was sponsored by the "Christian Business Men, and Pastors Churches in the Unadilla Valley where, as you recall, I grew up. I really enjoyed going to these suppers and hearing the different speakers. In the summer months, they would sponsor "old fashion tent revivals." They were fun, with folding chairs and sawdust on the ground. In fact I went forward and accepted Christ at one of these meetings. My uncle, Ernie had sponsored the tent meetings. He was the one that had married Arthur Welches' daughter Elrina, and had gone to Bible College. One of the men I met was Mr. Onie Odgden. He had a farm just up the road about four miles from us. He not only had a farm, but a saw-mill. It was about two weeks after I met him that he broke out in a severe skin disorder and could not milk his cows. I am not sure whether he came down to Clyde Head to ask him if I could help, or if he asked me directly. I do remember talking with Clyde. He stood behind me knowing that I could do it, even knowing that I had to change high schools in my senior year. I moved up on the Ogden farm into a duplex house. One side of the house was mine. It was very big for a young senior in high school! I milked 60 cows, cleaned the barn, washed the milking machines, cleaned up a bit and went to school. After school, I had the same routine. Saturday's, I cleaned up the barn in areas that I did not have time to do on a regular basis. I also went to the woods with the "little" John Deer bulldozer and wagon to cut firewood for the kitchen stove. When spring came, school was an option again. I did the plowing, disked, and dragged for two weeks. I was able to plant the oats, plus a small field of wheat. I planted the corn after the evening chores were finished each evening. All this meant that I had missed a total of 10 more days of school. Total 40 days of school missed, plus changed high schools all in my senior year. I did graduate that year, in June of 1961. It was also, the same year that "Uncle Sam" wanted me very badly. President Kennedy was very much at work in those days. I do remember that after I came back from the recruiting station in Oneida, NY, Mr. Ogden shared with me how he could keep me from having to serve Uncle Sam. He told me that after he had the papers drawn up by the lawyers, I would sign, and I would give him a good portion of the milk check, until the farm would be finally mine. These papers would exempt me form having to serve in the Army.

I knew that the hay was ready to harvest, bale, and put in the barn. He also had lumber that he was cutting for another farmer.

There was a burden of getting a hired man immediately to work the farm. All of this was on my mind as well. I loved working the farm and he knew that.

I was also thinking, I would never go to college if I accepted his deal. At least in the Army, I would get an opportunity to get some college and serve my country. My uncle, Cliff had served in the Navy and at this time our country had a motto, "ask not what your country can do for you, ask what you can do for your country." This sure sounded like a better deal to me.

Here we go, U. S. Army!!

9

MY SERVICE TO UNCLE SAM

It was August 1961 when I drove up to the Stone farm. I gave my keys and registration for the Cadillac to Patti. Then Patti, and her dad and I went to Syracuse, New York so that I could board the plane to Ft Dix. It was a couple of hours after that when my plane left for Fort Dix, New Jersey. I remember the first thing that happened when I arrived with some other boys, that the sergeant yelled, "Welcome to my world. Forget your mother; I'm your mommy now!" We then proceeded to the main building where we gave up our clothes, for uniforms; they then put us in showers and made sure everybody had a good clean shower. We put our uniforms on, got our heads shaved, teeth checked, feet checked, and proceeded to another building where we received a "mess" of shots. Welcome to Uncle Sam's camp! Boot Camp was eight weeks long, and very brutal!! We were training as replacements for Germany. (Mop up duty). They informed us that hand-to-hand combat was a major part of our training. We were not to take it lightly! We had much out-door foxhole training. ("Biv-wacking, etc") We also learned to get through the barbed wire in full gear. One of the things I enjoyed was the rifle training. I guess it was because we always hunted on the farm, so this was a bit more fun for me. I did very well in it! After boot camp, I was able to go home on leave for two weeks before going to my new station. They first told us everyone was heading to Germany. However, they pulled out thirteen of us, because we had taken typing in high school and would be going elsewhere. My orders were to go to Fort Lee Virginia for cook school. The problem was that after being there for three weeks (in school) they told me that my orders had changed. I was supposed to be back in Ft. Dix, New Jersey. So, I went back there and finally graduated top honors of the class! My next assignment was Niagara Falls, New York, In the Missile Detachment. It was part of the of Bell-Aircraft base. We did coordination with the Air Force.

This was an Air Force Base. There were a total of five underground missile sites up in that area. But before I went there, I went to Madison, New York to spend some time in that area with family, friends, and Patti. We had a good time. Patti was a student at Houghton College then. This worked out well, because after the holidays, she and her cousin Carlene had to go back to college. This was about one hour from where I had to go. Her Uncle Cart and Aunt Carol had planned, on taking Patti & her cousin Carlene back. Therefore, I asked if there was room for a young, "soldier boy" to ride along. They agreed, and I rode with them as far as Leroy, New York, (a town located near Batavia.) From here I found the bus station, and got the bus to Buffalo, and then to Niagara Falls where I took a taxi to the base. I soon realized that things were a bit different on an Air Force base. There were thirteen of us Army men on an Air Force Base! I must tell you that they treated us "royally!" The Army allotted us a 40- passenger bus to use plus a staff car. We needed transportation from one missile site to the other, plus back and forth from one side of the airbase to the other. Since I had a commercial license already I, was given the bus responsibility. I took Army and Airforce men back and forth to the Niagara Falls 3-4 nights a week. I used the staff car once a month to go to Fort Niagara where I did our payroll. Occasionally I would drive the Warrant Officer out to one of the Missile sites. I enjoyed being here on this assignment. I was also able to go home almost every weekend and sometimes down to Houghton College to visit Patti.

It was along here that Patti's brother Fred was getting married to a girl in Florida. Her name was Barbara. Patti's parents wanted to go down for the wedding. Her brother Duane would take them down. The only problem was…the farm, the two younger brothers Jim and Carl, and grandma Austin. I had some leave time coming, so I took a week's leave, came home on the farm and with Jim and Carl kept the farm going. Carl was just a kid at this time. Patti took charge in the house with Grandma Austin and her three younger sisters, Kathy, Bobbie, and Nancy. It gave Patti and I a chance to see how family life really worked! We all survived!!

I do remember that in 1962, Our Missiles came above ground and we went on "Red Alert." This happened because two Russian Mig fighter jets had come across our northern no fly zone. This was the same night that I had planned on going down to Houghton College to see Patti. I had a diamond ring, and planned to ask her to be my wife. I did it anyway! She accepted and I was overjoyed. I was and still am deeply in love with her! It was shortly after this that a big change came. I received orders to go to Thule, Greenland. When my warrant officer found out, he proceeded to make orders for me to go to school in Fort Ben Harrison, Indiana. We waited for three weeks and finally I received my orders to go there to Headquarters Administration School. This was college level training that I had hoped to receive. In fact, it was fully accredited. With my eight-week course of eight hours a day, plus on the job training it equaled two years of college. My warrant officer said, "It will be fast, hard, and difficult; but I think you can do it." As it turned out, I did finish the course. Forty-eight started the course and only twenty-seven of us actually finished. Then, I headed back to Niagara Falls.

After a few months, I received orders again. This time to Korea! My warrant officer again advised me that he was going to be in the process of getting the overseas orders changed. Two weeks later he handed me orders to go back to Fort Ben Harrison, Indiana. This time, it was for a computer, training course of eight weeks, and another equivalent to two years of college, with the adding on of the hands on experience. There were thirty-seven of us from seven different bases that were to get training on the new 1401 Honey-well computer processor. I remember seeing it for the first time. It took up almost a whole room. It had big thirteen-inch discs for information. Back then, the computer discs were sent to various locations around the states. To make a long story short I did graduate from the training. It was very difficult! Eight hours a day, six days a week for eight weeks! All thirty-seven of us expected orders to go to Paris, France. However, only 15 or so graduated and those that went to Paris came back early as France shut the door on US troops. Three of us received orders to go to Fort Meade, Maryland. I was very happy! I had a two-week leave, so I went to Madison, New York. It was toward the end of my first week there on the farm with Patti, that she approached me about our marriage plans. We had decided before this to get married the following February when she finished her college. Now, she and her mother thought that maybe it would be better to have the wedding in the good weather. Fast plans, went into effect. Yes! We were married the following Friday night. It was August 9th, 1963. WOW! I had my lovely wife Patti, and our 1956 Ford convertible, man…this was living! We had our honeymoon in Niagara Falls. I was able to show Patti many places there, since that is where I was last area of service. We had a great weekend! The following Monday morning I left for Fort Meade, Maryland, and Patti went back to finish her nurses training in Cortland, New York. I arrived at the base in Maryland and it was about 1:00p.m. It was 101 degrees. HOT! I was not used to the high humidity. My company commander told me after reviewing my orders that they did not need my service. He told me that they had government G.S.I.S. employees that did that particular job. He proceeded to find me another M. O. S. (mode of service). One issue that he faced was the fact that I only had thirteen months of service left. To start a new M.O.S., I needed two years. The next day I went back to his office and found out that he had a plan laid out for me. Since I had a military license, and had Headquarters Administration training, I was qualified for the job that he had. It was quite, unique! I would be working with one my previous warrant officers and a team that was being put together on a secret project. I would be in the office there at Ft Meade some of the time and driving him around part of the time. As it turned out, I drove him to the Pentagon each Monday, Wednesday, and Friday. I would work on the Army morning reports: All those sick; those that received promotions; doing all the necessary changes, and then I gave out the mail to different offices. I also, processed and sent the new troops over-seas to Vietnam. I thought it was a fun job. Then, I found out what was really happening over there Afternoons the team worked on the project.

Tuesday, and Thursday of each week, I went to the office, cleaned it, sorted the mail, answered the telephone. I usually only had to be there from 9:00 until 11:00; and from 2:00 until 3:00. On those two days I was home by 4:00p.m. I got a job not far from the base. I was a short order cook! The hours were from 5:00 until midnight, or whenever I could get away. I was able to use my cook school training that Uncle Sam had given me. I invented the "double" cheese burg, submarine sandwich. I sold a lot of them. I enjoyed this last part of my military time. I was looking forward to getting out of the military. Patti had joined me in Maryland by January 1964 and she really did not like the military life. She did not like the high humidity in Maryland either. It was different to say the least.

My discharge papers were supposed to come down to me in another week. I was very nervous whether they would or not let me out because Vietnam had been in full swing for two years by then. I had sent many from the Pentagon where I worked. We had many soldiers go over there. I went and had my discharge physical and all my discharge items taken care of just in case I could leave. I went in to the company Commander's office, and was told, by him that I could be discharged but I would be placed on inactive service for three years. This meant that they could call me anytime during the next three years. I had two weeks sick pay, and two weeks leave pay coming as my severance package. I traded in the '56 Ford convertible because it had almost 200,000 miles on it. I bought a 1958 Oldsmobile super 88 2-door Coupe. It was black with a white top. It was a very nice car. It was going to be different for me to be out of the military.

Patti and I left the next day for a nice "first" anniversary trip up to the Thousand Islands! We had a great time! When we got back to Madison, New York, we wondered what was next for us. As long as we were together, we were ready for whatever life would bring! WHAT WOULD IT BE???

10

FROM TURMOIL TO PEACE!

I was happy to be out of the military, but it was time to see about a job. I had a wife to keep happy and I needed something to keep me occupied. I remember that somehow I received word about a job down in Kingston, New York that I might want to check out. I left on the third Monday of August for Kingston.

I made the appointment, and then they took me around the place. They were looking for someone that had training and had worked in a Headquarters Department. I was given some tests to accomplish and finished by 11:30a.m. They told me to go to lunch and come back about 2:00p.m. I did just that, and later when I came back they told me I had the job. It was quality control, and I was to start the next Monday morning. I picked up a local newspaper so Patti could find an L.P.N. job because she wanted to work as well. Everybody was excited about my new job, and we were packing up the car to head out the next Sunday afternoon.

There were some mixed emotions however. You need to know that the job was Located in Kingston, New York at the Hudson Dynamite Company. As quality control, my particular job was to inspect the dynamite sticks. I had to make sure that none were crimped on the edge before they were packed. The operators stood behind a thick, steel frame, in which is a small hole that they place their hand into, carrying a dynamite casing. They placed the stick in the holder and then pulled a lever that came down into the case filling it and pressing the dynamite powder stick. They had a mirror to look at above their head that showed them exactly what was happening. If there was any damaged, I had to mark it down and place it in my steel recycling box. They have never had an explosion in this department. If I did my inspections correctly on the machine, the cases and the personnel were safe.

The only real hazard was the bent sticks! I was to keep them in the steel vault until Saturday. On Saturday, they assigned another person with me to go to the Hudson River nearby. Here, we placed the blasting cap into them then threw them down over the cliff into the river and "blew them off" I not only got time-and-a half, but also hazardous duty pay. I was making good money at that time of my life. In October 1964, we came home for a weekend. I took the car up to Lewis Oldsmobile in Waterville, New York to get something checked out. While I was there, the '65 Oldsmobile was on the show room floor. I was looking at them as the manager came over. He talked me into a brand new leftover '64 Oldsmobile Dynamic 88. It was very nice, a four-door hardtop and loaded. We were doing all right! Nice jobs, new car, and did I mention that Patti was expecting? Yes, we were going to have a baby!

The job was going great, and we liked it there. Thanksgiving was different for us because Patti could not get the time off for us to go back home. She worked 11:00p.m. - 7:00 a.m. the night before thanksgiving as they did not have enough help. I went ahead and cooked the whole Thanksgiving dinner while she slept. I cooked the turkey, made rolls, pies etc. My cook training in the army paid off after all. We had a very nice Thanksgiving together when she awoke at 4:00 p.m.

Something different for Patti and I was the big shopping Mall down in Kingston. She was working, and with my job, it was nice to be able to shop! We noticed that in the Montgomery Ward Store they had three dolls, a tall one, medium height one and a short one all dressed in red and white for Christmas. These dolls were just about as tall as Patti's sisters, Kathy, Bobbie, and Nancy. Boy, were her sisters going to

like them! We decided that we would buy them! We really were excited
when they came down that Christmas morning and opened their presents. What a Christmas! The holidays just went by too fast and it was
time to go back to work.

When I arrived back at the job, I was ushered into a meeting. The
government had a contract in Mexico. That contract had now been
cancelled. All of us who were hired last summer were out of work as of
the next Monday. Boy, things sure can change in a hurry! With a new
car, and a baby on the way, I started looking for a job immediately.
Sure, I know they told me I could get some sort of unemployment, but
not much, since it was for only six months. I refinanced with General
Motors Financing. I lost my '64 Oldsmobile, and received from them
a '60 Cadillac Fleetwood Brougham, gold in color. It was a very nice
car, though.

Since I always had a commercial license, I found a job that wanted
me to start Monday. Perfect! It was driving taxi in Kingston, New York!
The job was not bad at all. I got the hang of it, and local maps got me
around okay. The clients were not a real nice people. You could not
please them for anything. I decided to look for something else. Lord,
what's going on?

Patti and I came home for the weekend. It was the first weekend
of March. I was at the barbershop, and noticed a sign, which read,
"Wanted, someone to do field work." It was the McCormick farms in
Waterville, New York. Tractor work was what I liked to do. I went over
to see them for an interview. I got the job and could start in the following week. We headed back to Kingston. We took Kathy, Patti's sister,
with us to help Patti pack. While we were packing, we decided to take
Kathy that Saturday to see a movie that we noticed in the paper. The
name of the movie was "Mary Poppins." She loved it! That following
Saturday we moved back to the home area, Waterville, New York. It
was a cute little house!

The job at the McCormick farm started at 5:00 a.m. There was
milking to do; then the basic chores and getting the machinery greased
for the day. After breakfast, I went out into the fields as soon as possible.

The McCormick farms were scattered over the back roads of the town of Waterville, plus some land in Oriskany Falls, New York. We grew hay and corn for the cows; then potatoes, broccoli, and cabbage as cash crops, we kept busy preparing the soil, planting, then cultivating, and finally harvesting. It was during the cultivating time that our first child, Patsy, decided to come into the world. What a beautiful baby! She came home from the hospital in that nice gold Cadillac! However, my job here was about over, since the cash crops were harvested now. They failed to tell me that it was just a summer job.

The next place of employment was at the George Keith farms where I would take care of the chores on the upper farm, plus help out on the main farm. The old house had a wood furnace in it, so I had to cut a lot of wood as well. Patti was expecting again, and I needed her to be warm. It was here our son, Troy, was born! One day while I was on my way back from the main farm, the transmission went out on the Cadillac, causing major damage to the motor as well. I was able to get an old '52 Ford from one of the neighbors quite cheap. It was a three-speed-stick and very reliable according to them. I bought it. At least we had a car. Shortly after this, one day I arrived over at the main farm when George told me that there was a fire at our home. Patti had called him, so we rushed over there and it took us awhile before we got the fire out. It had scorched up the under-floor terribly, and the water damage was bad. I remember thinking that maybe God was trying to get my attention. Sure, we were going to church, but not more than the Sunday morning thing. Patti's folks let us stay there while we put the house in order, but I did not like it there on the Keith farm at all.

The following spring, I heard about a nice big farm down in Hubbardsville, New York, called the Lambhurst farm. They also wanted someone to do field work. We moved down to the old Wickwire Farm, which my boss owned, (he had heifers there as well). It was a nice quiet place on a dead end road away from all the hustle and bustle, nice for the two children.

Winters proved interesting as college kids from Colgate College liked to go up the dead end road just a bit and park. In the winter many times they would get stuck in the middle of the night, knock on our door. I would have to get dressed and get the tractor and pull them out. I usually got $10 for this fun time in the middle of the night.

Erwin Lamb was now, incorporated. He had built one of the biggest pole barns around at that time. The silos were huge! I realized this when Erwin and I went up to the top of each of the silo's and shimmed out to where we would bolt down the legs of the silo un-loader as the crane raised it up to us. We were about 70 feet in the air, and the silo's, were 40 feet across. There would definitely be a lot of corn! In fact, we had cornfields that went for miles and when we planted on the flat fields, we would double-plant corn. We would plant down one row, turn around and plant again two inches apart. It was fun chopping because you could get a load of corn fast, since instead of chopping two rows, you actually were chopping four. I really liked the field and tractor work.

One Sunday, Patti's brother Jimmy asked me in church if he thought he could get a part-time job there. I asked Erwin and he hired Jimmy right away. Jimmy would be helping with the cows; milking, feeding etc. He came to our house for supper quite often. He knew that I went to Brookfield School at one time when I was on the Clyde Head farm. He asked me if I knew of a certain girl from there by the name of Sherry Maine. I told him I knew her folks because they were neighbors to Lawrence and Anna Baldwin who were my parents' friends. He said he really liked her and talked to her once. Well, Patti and I went over to her place and talked for awhile one evening, and we made a date for her to come to our house to meet Jimmy. The night came when this was to happen and Patti and I went and picked her up. By the time Jimmy had done chores, we were back home. They enjoyed the supper and from there it was history. They have been married many years now with a big family!

Patti and I went to Hamilton, New York to shop at the grocery store just as we had many times before. Each week we went by the Trask dealer car lot. We spotted a nice little Buick there, one of the small models. It was a '63 Buick special with a small engine. We tried it out and bought it. The old Ford was getting to be not so reliable anymore and this was nice.

There was one big problem in my life. ME! It seemed that I was not really at peace with myself. I wanted this and that, but did not have any real peace. I liked the fieldwork and I liked the house, but maybe I needed to get what I thought was a "real" job, so I found one.

I hired out at the Grand Union Store, where I trained to be a journeyman, meat cutter. This was what I thought to be a "real job" at 40 hours a week. Patti was also working. Then we moved into an apartment in Oriskany Falls, New York. The job I had cutting meat meant that I would be filling in for meat managers all throughout central New York. I would need something cheaper for myself to drive. I bought 1 '62 Volkswagen Convertible, red with a black top. It was cheaper to run and it was a nice car. When I came home one night, Patti told me that we were going to have another child. We soon realized that Patti's little Buick was too small. While we were up in New Hartford, New York on a date one Friday night we came across a '67 Ford Country Squire station wagon. It was a demonstrator with less than 3,000 miles on it. This would be a good family car. As it so happened, I had worked a lot of over-time, plus I had two weeks vacation coming, we decided to go to Cape Cod. Patti also wanted to see her best friend from college. So off we went! There were Patti and I, with Patsy, Troy and Carla... to be born in a few months. We went to Philadelphia, Pa. To see Trish and Phil Brunozzi, and from there went to the Cape. It was a great trip. This was the first time we had a vacation since I got out of the military. Carla was born in February she was so tiny! My family was growing! Apartments were a bit too small!

I continued working for Grand Union, on the road, for about three years until a change was about to happen. A new manager took over the Oneida, New York store where I cut meat. His name was Edward Whitehead. He liked to kid with me a lot because I had a '64 Ford convertible now!

One day while on break, Ed and I were talking, and I found out that he was a pastor. I am telling you that God has a sense of humor, putting this man in my path at this time of my life. He told me that he was looking for a small country church that could not afford a pastor, but wanted one. Now Patti and I were active in our church. We sang together in the choir, also sang at weddings and different events at the church. We taught Sunday school, I was also a deacon. Since Pastor Card had left, I had been serving on the pulpit committee. I told Ed all of this. That Wednesday night after prayer meeting, I held a pulpit committee meeting. All were in favor of having him come when he could, and I relayed the message to Ed the next day. He told me he would be with us Sunday all day. They people of the church loved him! Monday, Tuesday, and Wednesday, his wife, Pat, and the children came in the store to visit me. On Wednesday night, the church took a vote. The results were turned in and he was elected to be our next Pastor. Thursday morning, Ed's whole family, was there when I arrived at the store. When I told them the good news there was a great time together! [That was over 40 years ago, and Ed is still Pastor at the North Brookfield Baptist Church.]

Patti and I purchased a home from Gene Beach, the owner of Kling's Mills in North Brookfield. It was the home that Patti's parents had started their lives in. It also was the home where my Grandma and Grandpa Clemens lived when I was a kid. (You will remember me talking about this in a previous chapter). It was a nice house, up a long driveway, along the railroad tracks and next to the Nine mile Swamp. We had not been there very long when Patti landed a nursing job at St. Luke's hospital near Utica, New York. She would need a newer car now. We went up to a Ford dealership in New Hartford, and bought her a brand new '70 Maverick with 26 miles on it. We paid $2,595 for it. It would be a less expensive car for her to drive, and reliable for her working from 11:00p.m.-7:00a.m. The new house was a bit farther for me to drive, but I did not mind. There was a brand new Grand Union store opening up, in Dewitt, New York, and I was getting much overtime there. However, two weeks after we bought the house, they told me that they were going to give me a permanent position there. That meant no more travel pay and no more overtime. I was to be there in this store, period! My concern was, regarding the long drive to work now, and without all the extra money, I did not think I wanted that job. I had a '64 Ford Galaxy convertible with a 390 v-8 engine that I was driving and it was not very good on gas. I had a lot of fun with it but my paycheck would go up in gas!

In the meantime, I walked a short distance, over the railroad tracks to Kling's Mills for something I needed for the house at his hardware store. Gene, the owner, asked me if I wanted to drive truck and work for him. I told him that I would come back in a couple of days to start, and he told me the truck would be ready for me. The next day I arrived at Grand Union and told them I was finished and to send me my check. They were not happy!

Do you remember me talking about the church, and our new pastor, Ed Whitehead? They liked the church parsonage. A lot had happened in just a week or two! The Whitehead children and our children were about the same age. We did many family things together. Gene, my boss told me that I would have a lot more than forty hours a week. He shared with me something that he thought might help me. He had to take out a lot of taxes from my pay because off the hours of overtime. The hours of overtime would not help me much since he had to the taxes out. He had a notebook for me to use to keep track of my over time. I also would help him with the billing now and then, so we both would know about my extra hours. Patti and I were remodeling our house. He knew that we would have need of a lot of things for the house. If we bought them, they would be expensive. I would put my overtime hours down in the book, and when I needed anything for the house, the price came off the hours in the book, not out of my check! Nice! We bought most of the items that we needed. One of these was Patrician Cabinets for the kitchen. Another was a copper tone side-by-side refrigerator/freezer. Also, we got paneling for the living room. Patti's father, her brothers, cousins, and people from the Church all helped us. The people from the North Brookfield Baptist church were really a nice spiritual family!

We loved the Whitehead family. Patti and I had purchased a two room family tent so we as a family could go camping and spend some good time together as a family. While talking to Pastor Whitehead, he mentioned that they also had one, and that we ought to go camping together sometime. This was something that both of our families liked to do. We spent many Friday nights and Saturdays together in the summer months.

We also, both had Baptist Life Insurance for our families and noticed that in July they were having a family camp up at the Canandaigua Lake. We signed up and went, although Patti tells me, "We are going to have another child." WOW! Think of it, four children? Well, Kandi was born! Four months after she was born, we all went to the camp. The Whiteheads, and their family would be in their two-room tent and our family would be in our two-room tent. When we arrived at the camp, we found out that our tents would be way up on the side hill overlooking the lake. It was absolutely the most beautiful place! The kids program, the music, the food, and the fellowship outstanding! The special speakers were also good. I remember one of them spoke about a Bible college where married couples could go. I could work days and go to college at night. It also had a very strong mission emphasis. Now I had forgotten about the Watkins and their mission endeavor, so this really got my attention!

Plus, I did not have peace with myself! They challenged us to come forward if we had any drawing of the Holy Spirit to do so. I went up and surrendered my life for His service wherever He wanted me, but please Lord, not a pastorate! We went back home changed and waited for another chapter in our lives to begin. We knew that God was at work in our lives. We had surrendered to serve Him and we were waiting for Him to open a door for us to go through. In the meantime, we served the Lord in our home church. I thought I would be able to save a nest egg of money so it would not be so hard when we went to Bible College.

We knew that God never would lead us but what His grace would sustain us. Praise His holy name!

I had been running from the Lord since I graduated from high school. I knew God wanted me to go to Bible College, but I ran!

This must be pray and preparation time for me, and my family. We will use it to examine our call to serve Him, and we will prepare ourselves for whatever He has in store. No more running!

11

OUR CALL TO SERVE GOD!

Something was definitely different in our lives. In church I talked with Pastor Ed and he told me to just go ahead and try some doors that God may be opening, and see if God opened or closed them all. I remember that Patti and I applied to three Bible colleges: Practical Bible Training School, Seaway Baptist College, and Elohim Bible College. All three Bible colleges accepted us! Since Elohim was set up and designed for married couples, we decided to go there. My classes were at night from 7:00-10:00p.m, and Saturday mornings from 8:00a.m.-noon. This allowed us to work during the day.

We decided that we would attend the following year. This would give us time to set aside some funds for college. However, one day that winter, I broke all five bones in my wrist while getting off the truck. My wrist had to be "fused" with five pieces of bone graft from my hip, (sort of like a welding job.) Our plan for extra funds, versus our trust in God, was my first lesson in following Him. I was on a limited disability income. It was a very painful operation, yet I had much time to spend with my family. That summer we sold our house back to Gene Beach, and we moved up on the farm where Junior Head used to be. Patti's cousin Ron Head bought this farm and he allowed us to use the house until we left for Bible school. It was a big house with a swimming pool, and since I had one of the new plastic casts on, I was able to swim in the pool. We sold both of our cars and purchased a blue '70 Chevy Nomad Wagon. It was at this time in my life, that I gave my life to God for missions. I was thinking, it would be somewhere in the United States.

We moved to Castile, New York to begin Bible School that August of 1973. I drove our furnishings out with one of the same trucks I used to drive for Gene. While at college, my 1st job was driving truck for Rich Plan Foods. However, I missed a lot of my 1st class at school. I then got a job doing field and tractor work for the McCormick farms, not far from the school. It was a cash crop farm. Potatoes were one of the biggest crops. It was interesting to me that Mr. McCormick had a contract made with the Wise Potato Chip Company, before he even planted the potatoes. The job was with bigger and newer tractors than I had ever used before! I soon realized that once the crops were all harvested in the fall that my job was finished. There would not be any check from unemployment since I would not have enough months to qualify. Our budget was very tight!

We learned another lesson of God supplying our needs. We only had some oatmeal left in the house and a few dollars left in our pockets. We went to prayer meeting, giving God all we had, and shared with them that we were learning how God supplies.

The next night was Thursday a class night. After class, we came home from school and when we turned into our driveway, we noticed there were some bags in the front entryway. We soon discovered that they were full of groceries! WOW! God had answered our prayers and supplied our need. The following Sunday we were sharing in Sunday school, and found out that an older couple had bought the groceries, then came on our street where three houses of married students lived. They stopped the car in front of our house, asked God which place to give the groceries and God seemed to be telling them to leave the groceries right there. (Wow our home)! Thank you Jesus for supplying our needs!

I had many jobs throughout my three years in school. I worked there on the farm, trimmed trees at an apple orchard, sealed plastic tarps at the plastic factory, and served at the local hospital as an orderly. God always provided a job each time a place laid-off or closed down. At Bible College I learned many lessons and much about God's Word. We worked at an A.W.A.N.A. camp in Brakney, Pa. for two summers. Patti was the nurse and I taught counselors in training. We seemed to have a wonderful time with the youth.

I think one of the greatest lessons was that of the importance of missions. It was in our second year of Bible College, that Patti and I had an assignment of learning about the people and the culture of any country that we felt the Lord wanted us to do. We both decided to do our study on the Philippine Islands. It was a real eye opener for us and we were very interested in those people. We found out a lot! Now it is interesting how God puts things all together! Each month there was a missionary speaker that came for our chapel time. One really got our attention. First, he asked if any one knew a missionary. Yes I did! I was a real good friend with the Watkins family in Africa, and I remember them well. Then he asked if any of us had ever done a study on the culture and people of a foreign field. Yes we had! We felt challenged and led of the Lord to go forward that night answering the call to missions. The next evening he came to our house and visited. Then he had Patti go upstairs, and had me go into the bedroom. We were to pray and ask God to have us write down on paper a country that we may want to consider going to for mission work. It was obvious that we both had put down the Philippines. Soon the application was in progress at the mission office.. We later learned that we were accepted to go to the Philippines as missionaries!

After graduation in June 1976, we packed up and left for missionary candidate school. There were about 20 candidates there. Only seven completed the candidate school. We then came home to Madison, New York for the summer and winter. During this time Pastor Whitehead and the North Brookfield Baptist Church called "an Ordination Council" for me. There were seven different pastors, including one that I did not know. His name was Kenneth Rogers from Berean Bible Church in Greene, New York. In fact he volunteered to be the moderator for me that day and did an excellent job. I passed the ordination and he asked if I would come to speak at his church. I reserved a date with him.

During our time of deputation, we lived in Madison, New York, where I also cut meat for an income in two different stores. One was in North Brookfield, owned by Pastor Ed Whitehead. However, the store closed after a few years. The other store, Quinn's market, was in Sherburne, New York. The owner died and his son took over and needed a meat cutter. The meat department needed a boost. It was bringing in less than $800.00 a week. After one year of working there, we were doing $2100.00 a week in that meat department! It was fun! Now, the manager gave me a chance to own the store if I wanted it. I would only give him a portion of the percentage each week. I realized that Satan always wants to test our faith. I told him thanks a lot but our main business was going around trying to raise support to go to the Philippine Islands, as missionaries.

While going from church to church, Pastor Rogers wanted Patti and I to be in their upcoming mission's conference in the Berean Bible Church. We had a great time and even had a meeting with the youth. After the youth meeting and the bon-fire with the youth on Friday night, Pastor Rogers asked me to come into his office. It was there that he told me that the youth wanted to know if Patti and I would come and work with them. He had called the deacons and all were in favor.

WOW! We would have a ministry here and use this church as our home church. I said, "Yes!" Pastor Rogers then told me that Berean Bible Church would be taking us on for support. I would be working with the teens and leading the first part of the worship services. I would also have a chance to preach occasionally, and do visitation. This was exciting for Patti and I! The church treated us very well! Pastor Rogers took me under his care, and that year helped me develop into a full missionary. There were those who said that with four children, it could take four to five years to get to a foreign field. We made a target date of when the best time to leave for the field would be. We began to pray the Lord's will. At the end of June, we felt that God gave us a specific

date in August to leave for the field. Pastor Rogers and his wife, Patti &
I all began to fast and pray. With God's grace, we were able to leave for
California in two years! We had two churches in Nebraska that wanted
us to stop by. One of those churches also took us on for support, and
the other gave us a love offering that got us to California. We made it
from Nebraska to California in two days. That was very tiring. Our
children had mixed emotions about driving across the United States
anyway but that was hard on all of us.

The following day we received all our shots, and then sold the car,
and met Bob and Grace Kohler. They had been missionaries in the
Philippines for many, many years. We all made it to the airport on
time. We had all our paperwork completed and got on the plane leaving for Hawaii, where we took the international flight to the Philippine
Islands. WOW! What a full and exciting day! We left California about
5:15 p. m. and we will be in Manila Philippines about 5:00 tomorrow
evening.

A new experience is in store for us!

12

CULTURE SHOCK!

Our first question after landing in Manila was, "What are we doing here?" The Heat and the humidity were a shock to us! While getting our luggage off the airplane, we realized our daughter Carla's luggage was not there. We then informed the airlines that Carla's luggage was missing. After that, was the mad hustle and bustle of people all trying to get the same "Jeepney," or taxi. The Jeepney is an old military jeep that has the frame cut, with an extended long frame put into it. They can carry 20-25 people on it. They have long, open seats and plastic, which folds down when it is rainy. We also saw these men with bicycles that had sidecars on them which carried 5-6 people. Now this was something else to see. Such was the public transportation system here in the Philippines. It was fortunate for us that we had a ride with some missionaries who had their own transportation.

The next few days we spent buying some clothes for Carla, and taking care of paper work at the Philippine Embassy and the American Embassy. Having them put in order, we made sure that they knew where we were going to be in their country. Three of our four children were going to be staying in Manila for missionary school. This was going to be very hard for Patti and me. Our youngest daughter Kandi, would be going down to another island called Mindanao, with us, where we would be church planting. It was already hard on us to think about leaving three of our children up there in Manila. It was also hard for an American to realize that the pace of life there is slow! Waiting for the public transportation and then the waiting lines at the offices, sure taught us patience!

The weekend came and we did a little sightseeing. It sure was different, yet it was beautiful in many ways. On Monday and Tuesday, we took Patsy, Troy, and Carla up to Faith Academy, where they would be attending school. We got them registered for their classes, and then we took each of them to their dorms and met the dorm parents. It was getting harder and harder on Patti and I at this point, yet we knew that there was not much for them down on Mindanao Island where we were going to be. We spent two weeks in Manila, acclimated ourselves to the climate and getting the children settled into Faith Academy.

The small jet that took us to Mindanao Island was nice. It held about 60 people. What a drastic difference there was on this island! The differences were not just the coconut palms, the forestry, and the primitive airport as well. WOW! This actually brought to my mind the '40's and '50's. The Philippine people just simply exist from day to day. They took us to the mission headquarters in an old Volkswagen Truck that the Kohler's owned! We met Ken and Melvine Heard, who were going to be our culture training persons. There were Filippino's all over their yard. Most of them were from the churches that Bob and Grace Kohler had started. They have been there for many years. We were then, introduced to many of their pastors. We also met the pastor where we would be worshipping and getting our language tutoring. This was all very different for Patti, Kandi and me. We became aware of the fact that our older children would not have liked this at all, although, we discovered that they did have Pepsi Cola. It was a bit sweeter than what it is in the States. The food was mostly rice dishes, since rice is the number one commodity on the island. Most of the foods they prepare with fish, chicken, or pork. It was fun to watch them put their food on a banana leaf and eat. Here in the city of Cagayan de Oro, where we lived, the meat was mostly fresh fish.

Language study was a lot of fun. Pastor Celez knew seven dialects and he was quite good. He would have us learn phrases in the morning, and go practice them in the open-air markets in the afternoon, after our siesta. In this hot humid weather, everyone took a siesta (a nap). It was fun in the market place. Now, the average American had a problem, because the people laughed when you tried to use their language. We were taught, very early that they were not laughing at us, but happy that we were trying to talk the Cebuano language that they used there. We learned how to do our shopping and get a few bargains in the process. English for me was a very difficult subject. However, in two years I was able to write enough of a sermon in Cebuano to get by.

It was about two weeks after we arrived, that the Ken Heard helped us locate our own house to rent. Then we bought all local furnishings. They actually do remarkable things with bamboo! Many of our things were made of this. After we had set up our home and moved into it, we met two college students, Ling, and Pat, who were sister's, that had been part of an existing church. One of the things about the culture is that you are supposed to have a house helper. Therefore, we hired these two girls to come live with us and help Patti with cleaning, laundry, and other errands. They were very bashful, yet seemed to like us. Two cultures were becoming one. I had a Cebuano Bible and one night as Patti, Kandi, and I were having devotions, with the girls, I read John 3:16 from the Cebuano Bible. Then each night after that, I would read the Romans Road from the Cebuano Bible. It was about the third night later that Ling had some questions regarding what we were reading. Patti and I led her to know Jesus as her Saviour. Wow! We confirmed what God was doing through us in the Philippines! Shortly after this, her older sister, Pat accepted Christ as her Saviour. This was so exciting! They really changed and were more open with us after that.

It was about this time that we decided to go up into the mountains and visit an orphanage there, we had heard about. It was in operation by an American. The orphanage was under the board of the Browncroft Community Church. We met one of the workers from the orphanage while we stayed in Cagayan De Oro. While we were there at the orphanage, they asked us if we would be interested in adopting. I heard them talking previously about two girls. So I said, "Only if it's a boy." They replied, "We have one." They informed me that he was very shy around men. However, when they brought him out he smiled at me and wanted to come to me as well. This was odd! The following Monday when they came to the city, they asked us if we would watch him. We did just that, and by the following week they were going to place him in our home! We named him Jason. He was six month's old. After the paper work, they asked our oldest daughter, Patsy, many questions since she was older and she had to approve the adoption as well. Finally, they approved us for Jason's adoption. This all happened within a three month period. We had to wait six more months, for the adoption to be legal. We now had another son!

We soon realized that Satan was not happy about the salvation of Ling and Pat. Patti and Kandi became very sick with Cholera. The symptoms were stomach cramps with nausea diarrhea, food would not stay down and they were very sick. This went on for about two weeks. The doctor told us that it was more than likely a reaction to the cholera shots which we all took before we left the States. We all prayed together each night during our devotions time. We thank God that he heard our prayers, and they were soon better.

Valentines Day came and Pastor Celez wanted me to speak at the college's Valentines Banquet. This was my first test before the nationals. The day before Valentines Day, we received word that Patti's dad died. What a shock! She actually received a copy of his obituary. You must realize that during that particular era, it took almost three weeks for us to get a letter from the U.S. There was absolutely nothing, we could do. Then, on top of this, it was Valentines evening, the night I speak! We were all dressed up for the banquet, and it was pouring down rain. It was hard enough that we had received the bad news of Patti's Dad, but then rain, dirt roads, and mud. Mud made it very difficult to walk over to the church. What a night! When we arrived at the church, we found that they had decorated very well. What caught our attention was not what we expected! The long table had plates of rice and fish, and there were three pigs' heads with their snouts up in the air with apples in the mouths! This was their special treat! Oh my, what a night!

It was also around this time that we took Ling & Pat up into the mountains to meet their family. We had a rough time going through the mud and across the river. It was a real "mountain experience". Once we got up there, the generator went bad in the Jeepney. Their dad and I had to go back down to the closest barrio to get the part that we needed. He knew about two words of English and I knew about 25 of words of Cebuano. We did get the part that we needed and got the Jeepney going again. Ling and Pat's family was very nice. During the course of the weekend, we were able to share the Gospel with them. They were receptive except for the mother, who spat on the floor while saying "Baptists." This situation was going to take much prayer! We started back home and on the way we stopped in the city of Gingoog. It was a nice little village and there was a Baptist church newly built. We met a man there who told us that only three people come occasionally. WOW! This could be an opportunity for a ministry. We went home praying about it, and then about two weeks later, we started packing. Yes, we believed that God wanted us to move to Gingoog City.

Pastor Celez had lined up a truck, and some men to help us move. We loaded up everything and arrived in Gingoog at a nice house that we found. It was owned by a doctor who was trained in the U.S.A. This house had three steps going up onto the veranda on both sides, and underneath the steps there was a pond with gold fish and carp. There were small steps and I was able to drive the motorcycle right into the living room and lock it up for the night. (Other wise it would be stolen, along with a lot of other things!) Culture shock 101!

There in Gingoog City, the electricity was only on for the day, usually 6:00 a.m. until 6:00p.m. It was also not reliable. We tried to keep food as cold as we could at night, which meant that we shopped for food daily at the market with everyone else. Since there was no electricity at night, this meant that there was no running water at night as well. We had a large plastic garbage can full of water in the shower with a dipper. We called this our "dip & splash" shower.

Let me share two little things we learned about the culture in the Philippines.

First, if, they borrowed something and had not returned it, then you must not need it. If you did, you would ask for it back.

Secondly, if you gave someone a Bible or something of any value, even though, you wanted nothing in return, then they would give you something, as well. We accumulated many chickens. Plus the fresh eggs and the fried chicken made us enjoy these aspects of Filipino culture.

The Cebuano Bibles that we gave them were being read, used in church, and used in home Bible Studies. (All for God's glory) We opened our home to college young people who knew some English. Now, with these Cebuano Bibles, they were learning. Our ministry here started to grow from our home and spread to the villages in the mountains around us. These home Bible Studies in the mountain villages would be future churches. It was not easy getting up to these places at all!

Christmas was upon us again and our children were home from their school in Manila. Ling and Pat, our two Filipina girls had witnessed to their two brothers, and Patti and I had been back up to their place many times. The village people promised to have a new bridge built across the river and we heard that it was completed. We all decided to take the girls back up to their home. I need to let you know that it was the rainy season from November until March. It rained hard all day and the night before we left. When we arrived at the river, we noticed that the bank on both sides had washed away with the bridge. The villagers were cutting down long coconut trees and trimming them. They raised them to the banks and then we had four of them spanning the river. While all of this was going on we grew hungry and ate our peanut butter sandwiches (spreading the peanut butter with Patsy's comb) since we forgot a knife. Next they put ropes around these long trees and fastened them together underneath. When they finished all this, they asked me to drive up to the trees lining the wheels up. They taper cut the trees and now wanted me to drive across the river. Patti and the children all got out and walked with the national's help. Meanwhile, there I was in the Toyota Land Rover 15-20 feet in the air, driving across coconut trees! Thanks to our God, we all made it! Thank you Jesus! While we were up in Side- Seven, Ling and Pat's dad, her brother, and two cousins accepted Christ as their Savior. The trip was worth it all! We learned about how to raise coffee, coconuts, bananas, papayas, and pineapple. We drank fresh coconut milk, tasted many different Filipino foods and had a great visit.

All of these new believers came down to the church service on Sunday, even though, it takes them all day to come and go home. They brought vegetables, fruit, chickens, and rice to the two young men staying at the church, which was their way of tithing. These two young men were in Bible training and would later go to Bible School. We did find a national Bible school up in the mountain that had been built by the Association of Baptists for World Evangelism. Ling and Pat really liked the school. They both went there, to learn how to be Bible women, or pastor's, wives.

The church planting work was really starting to blossom. We had home Bible studies in Side-Seven, Side-Two, here in Gingoog city and a new prospect in Telesion. Both Ling and Pat were attending Bible school. The two young men from our church were ready to go the next semester. The church had about 23 people coming regularly. It was soon time for us to leave for furlough.

We packed up, and put our things in storage, then caught a flight to Manila, where we proceeded to Faith Academy International School to get Patsy, Troy, and Carla. The following four days we spent getting our documents in order for the international flight to the United States. What a shock it was to discover that there was a new regulation given by the government that basically made all American adoptions hold for one full year, before they were allowed to take the child out of the country. Jason had only been with us 10 months at that time. We then went to the United States Embassy where we showed them all our papers, and asked what to do next. It was evident that we could not afford to live in Manila for two months, and it was very expensive to go back down to Mindanao since all our furnishings were in storage.

One of the United States Ambassadors came and asked me if I had ever been in the military. I told him I had been in the service during the

Viet Nam era. He then knew that I, had been bonded while in the U. S. Army to work at that time in the Pentagon. He wanted to know if I still knew my bond number, which I did! He had me put the number in a correspondence to the States. He told us to come back in three days, which we did. Much to our surprise, the United States government let us bring him out of the country "non status." This meant that he was not a citizen, but could apply for citizenship after he was with us in the U.S., for one whole year. We then had all the paper work in order and would be leaving the Philippines that next evening at 5:00p.m.

Our first stop was in Hawaii for immigration and re-entry to the U.S. We had to leave our papers at the desk and wait our turn. We waited and waited! I also kept seeing them, take what looked like our papers, and keep putting them back on the bottom of the stack. Our flight to California was going to leave soon! I saw one of the officials, come out of his office, and I proceeded, to very politely tell him our dilemma. He went over to the desk and found our papers. He then asked me how I had gotten a "non status" visa for Jason. I told him, and his reply was that his help at the desk did not know what to do with it because they had never seen one. They had discontinued that particular visa seven years prior, to that. Therefore, none of his help knew what to do with that particular type of visa. He did however grant us our visa!

We then had to leave immediately because the airplane was put on hold, for us. However, just before we boarded, the official came running with a new paper. It seemed that he had put the wrong date on the first one. We would have had to set on the tarmac in California for one whole day before entering the airport. What an interesting few days we had! God worked it all out, and we were on our way to New Jersey where God was preparing a new chapter in our lives

13

OUR FIRST FURLOUGH

We arrived safely in Wayne, New Jersey at the Mission Office. Some one had left a large Oldsmobile Custom Cruiser wagon for us to use. They also had an apartment there that was for one of the staff members. Since she was out of town for a few days, we stayed there for three days before heading up to Madison, New York, where we were with family for a while. Patti's mother's place was an old farmhouse in the country that had lots of running space for the children. It was nice to be home again! (Even though, at times we wondered about the church planting work going on in the Philippines.)

All of Patti's family, my mother, and her two sisters were all together that Sunday. We worshipped in our home church, North Brookfield Baptist, where Pastor Whitehead is still the pastor. That was nice. It was good to see Mom and my sister's, again.

Boy, did we have a great day together! All the American food you could eat, then an old fashion game of horseshoes. They all thought that our adopted son Jason was a "cutie" and he sure hammed it up! The neighbor's across the street from Patti's mom also had an adopted child and told us about how they were getting the proper papers for that child to become an American Citizen. We received information about this for Jason when we arrived in the U.S. However, we had to wait until we had been here in the states for one whole year before,

Jason, could be sworn in as a citizen. Jason would then be three years old.

That next Sunday we went to Berean Bible Church in Greene, New York. That was our commissioning church when leaving to go to the field. They wanted us to stay at the house of Pastor Rogers for a week, while he and his family were on vacation. One of the deacons there also had some information on housing in the Binghamton, New York area, not far from the church. This allowed us to be in our home church and to help A.W.A.N.A. It also helped the pastor as well. We loved it there!

Monday morning we looked at an old, but nice house on Lockwood Street. It was just what we needed. There were three bedrooms, a large kitchen, garage and porch. It was just two blocks from the parks and handy to everything that we needed, such as a car repair shop, K Mart, a pizza place, and a convenience store! God is so good! We had a car given to us, and a place to live and we were back into our home church where we started deputation. Some furnishings were in the home given with donations from people in the church, we were all set! The children were happy as well! They were able to go to the Central Baptist Christian Academy, which was not far away from us. This was where they attended before we left for the field. Their school bus picked them up on the end of our street.

Deputation had begun! We were to be at Berean Bible church that Sunday, then North Brookfield the next weekend. We had one Sunday off, and then Eaton Community Church, Unadilla Forks Baptist, Waterville Baptist, and then a house church our friends Duane and Carol Jennings had just started in the Cooperstown area. Deputation was not just the meetings Sunday morning and evenings, but the mission banquets, going to different homes for meals, and getting the children dressed up as well because we sang as a family for many of the meetings. This was a busy next few months! Not only did we have meetings on the weekend but A.W.A.N.A. on Wednesday evenings as well. Patsy was busy with soccer practices and games.

Fall and winter were just around the corner, and we had almost forgotten how cold New York gets! We found this out on the New Year's weekend when we were down in Middletown, New York. We had a great weekend there with those folks! They had doubled their attendance and had just finished their new building project. It was beautiful! However, that Sunday evening when we were ready to leave, it was twenty degrees below zero! It was so cold that the defroster in the olds station wagon could hardly keep the windshield clear to see. The station wagon had heaters under the front seats for the back. Patsy's feet still got frost bitten! It was a very cold winter in New York! Patti and I decided that the rest of the winter, we would set up our deputation meetings where it would be just me going. This would be easier on the children anyway, because of their schooling and activities.

It was sure nice when the warmer weather came! We could walk in the park and was soon able to have family picnics there. Our schedule for the spring and early summer was filling fast. We had been able to set the date for Jason's citizenship, in July, just before we headed back to the Philippines. People had already given us a few things to take back. We were storing them in our garage.

Since that particular weekend we did not have a meeting anywhere, and the weather was supposed to be very nice, we were going to have my sister and my mom come down to the park for a picnic. The children all loved the park and they loved Dorothy and Mom as well. Let me tell you it was a great day! Mom and Dorothy were going to come in July for Jason's "swearing in" ceremony. We also learned that the neighbors we had up in Madison (where we had lived) would be there with their adopted girl. She would become a citizen that day also!

Easter weekend we spent at Morrisville, New York. The church had been meeting in a 4-H building when we left for the field. They now had a new beautiful church. We had a good time with the folks there as well as Pastor's family. We all remembered how our two families (the children included), used to go house-to-house in Morrisville, giving out tracks and inviting people to the church services. Pastor Tom told me that day that he would be leaving the church there soon. He was a church planter, and since the church was a full-fledged church, they were getting ready to call their first full-time pastor and Pastor Tom would start a new group elsewhere. We understood this because we were church planters as well.

We had finished our deputation traveling, and took some time to just relax. We spent time with friends and loved ones. We put our belongings for the Philippines on the truck to California. We then finished packing up some things from the house. We spent the rest of our time with Patti's mom in Madison, New York. While we were at our home church in North Brookfield, we found out the Memorial Day Parade was in town. Jason loved the parade and all the excitement! After the parade, we took him to the gravesite where he saw many of the family members' graves. In June, we spent much time with my mother and Patti's mother. We had many picnics together and went many places site seeing. There were many mixed feelings about going back to the Philippines. We also spent many evenings with the Whiteheads in the church parsonage. We even helped them at the end of June in their Daily Vacation Bible School. The mixed feelings were stronger than ever! We wanted to go back to the field, but this was home!

July had come, and the day was upon us to go to Norwich, New York, where Jason would become an American citizen! While he and Patti were standing before the judge, the judge asked him if he knew the Pledge of Allegiance and Jason recited it to him. My sister and mom began laughing, and the judge swore him in laughing as he did so! Mom took us all to Pizza Hut for supper, and then back to her place where we had ice cream and cake. We said our "good bye's", knowing we had to leave that next week for the field.

The following Thursday, we said "good bye" to Patti's mom, Aunt Mildred, and other family members, and headed to New Jersey where we would spend one night before leaving for the field. It had been a busy, fun filled furlough, and now we were heading back to the Philippines for another "Pierce Adventure!"

"The eyes of the Lord are upon the righteous, and his ears are open unto their cry."

14

BIBLE STUDIES AND GOD'S PROVISIONS

When we stepped off the airplane in Manila, Philippines, we had forgotten how hot and humid the weather was! One of the other missionary families picked us up at airport and spent the night with them. We also spent some quality time with our children, knowing that the next day we had to get them settled into their dorms at Faith Academy. They had already visited Mindanao Island, down where Patti and I worked. They knew that there was not very much for them there on that Island. Therefore, they liked Faith Academy.

Patsy, Troy, and Carla, all met their dorm parents. They also met some of their friends from before, after which we toured the school with them, before heading back down to Manila where we spent the night. The next day we had to get our paper work in order at the Embassy, and purchase our tickets to fly down to Mindanao Island. We even had time to pick up a few "American treats" to take down with us. Jason and Kandi were sad to leave their brother and sisters, but also looked forward to having Patti home school them.

The small jet ride to Mindanao took just over an hour. The airport here was very small. There was another missionary couple there to meet us this time. We spent about a week with them before heading to the language school in Butuan. We wanted to have a more aggressive pattern in our Cebuano language.

We found a nice home there within walking distance from the school. We met other American missionaries there from New Tribes Mission. We received much help from them when our household furnishings came from the storage. I can still see Kandi, Jason, Mom, and Ling as they unpacked all our things! It was nice to set up our home for just awhile again.

Language study was alright but the formal language training, compared to the uneducated way that was used in the mountain work around the Gingoog area, created a bit of a problem. We went to Gingoog every weekend to be with those folks that we had worked with from the previous term. After six months of this, and listening to those God called us to work with, we decided to move back to Gingoog City. This is where God had called us. It was very cost effective when you consider that gasoline there was over $5.00 a gallon. (That was one of the reasons we brought a 360 Yamaha from the U.S. in our mission crates with us.)

Looking back, when we had that bike, I remember that Patsy and one of her "boy" friends John borrowed one of the other missionaries' motorbikes. They were on that bike and Patti and I were on the 360. We had gone to Surigao City to see Patsy's friends, the Miller twins from Faith Academy. It was a nice day trip of about 3 hours each way. We had fun going to their place and a good time with the Miller family.

On the way back, was an exciting time to say the least! The motorcycle that Patsy and John were using developed some problems and would not keep running. We were right in the mountains, on the Surigao side. This is where the rebels and the Philippine Army were having many fights. A Jeepney stopped and put the motorbike on it. They told Patsy and John to get into the front seat. Mom and I were to follow…with the lights off on our motorcycle. I said, "No way." I could not imagine my daughter up there without lights on!! We did not even know if they were rebels or not. Patti and I suspected that there were at least three or four in the Jeepney. They also drove with their lights off as well. I followed, and after about 45 minutes the Jeepney stopped and some of the men got off carrying their rifles and running up into the woods. Then the Jeepney turned his headlights on and we proceeded back home. What a scary adventure!! Each and every day we would ask God to put a hedge around us and protect us. He answers our prayers. Praise His Holy Name!!

It was good to get back into the church-planting ministry where God called us. We had a nice group of nationals coming to the Gingoog Baptist Church, and up at Side 7 where we had a group meeting in a home. The doctor, there in the city, had a beautiful home that they wanted us to rent. It was just what we needed, a nice fenced in yard, with a carport. The doctor had trained in the U.S., and her husband was the city's pharmacist. We then not only had a nice home, but a doctor and pharmacist as well. God is so good!

The next thing we wanted to accomplish was, go up to the Bible school to see how Ling and Pat were doing. Also, Melo one of the young men from Gingoog Baptist Church was there as well. We always liked going back up in the mountain since it was a bit cooler. This part of the mountain was where there was a Linguistic Headquarters' that was run by Americans. We stayed there in one of the cottages. When we left Gingoog we went to one of our outreaches in the mountain. A week earlier while at Side 7 after the service, Ling and Pat's mom told us that her daughters wanted her to come with us to the Bible School. We asked her if she really wanted to go and she said, "Yes!" Patti and I thanked God for His since of humor! We knew their Mom was not saved as of yet. Now, she was going up to see her daughters at the Bible School. We had everyone we knew praying for her salvation. Praise God, while there, she accepted Christ as her Savior the very night we arrived! Now the whole family knew Jesus!

Another highlight of that trip was meeting one of the young men who would graduate soon. He had a wife and two children, and was interested in a church. After we met with him and some of the Bible School Officials, we went back to Gingoog to pray regarding the matter. On our next visit up to the Bible School, we asked him if he was still interested. He told us he was, so we planned to move him back to Gingoog after graduation. I remember that it was exciting how we had Bible school students, and home Bible studies going on, and now we had our first Pastor! Those were exciting days.

The Heard family, where we had stayed with back when we first arrived in the Philippines, no longer were there as Missionaries. We found out that they left the field due to family situations.

They also had a house helper named Alice. We learned that she had married a young man who was a pastor, and they lived not far from us. We went to visit them and discovered that they had a group of believers and were building a small church for worship. They asked us to help them, and to visit and encourage them. The Lord had really blessed and the work had really moved forward, faster then we could have imagined.

One of the things regarding the Philippines was the fact that, everyone took a "siesta" (a nap) around noon each day. This was because of the heat. It was very necessary. I remember that on a particular Sunday we had come home from church, ate our lunch and laid down for our siesta. Normally we slept about 30 minutes. This particular Sunday we could not sleep very well. We only tossed and turned. I had felt the urge to go visit Alice and her husband. Fuel was very expensive and we only had about forty pesos and the Toyota Land Cruiser, since the motorcycle was broke down. Also, it was the last week of the month. Yet, I felt that God wanted us to go.

When we arrived there, they were not there, and the neighbor told us that they had taken their baby boy up over the mountain pass to the main road, expecting to hitch a ride to Gingoog City. Their son had been sick with a high fever for three days. I remembered where the path came out and met the highway because we had seen people standing there often. So, we headed back up the around the side of the mountain to meet them if possible. We asked God to intervene for them and their son. As we were coming around the corner where the path meets the road we noticed them just coming up through the tall grass. We discovered that the son was in very sick. We took him to the Gingoog

City Hospital where they immediately admitted him. When we arrived back home, Patti cooked extra food to bring to them and we took it to the hospital for them. We arrived home late, and we were exhausted, but we thanked God for how He worked all things out, and thanked Him that we could use what little we had left for the month to help them. It usually took three weeks for a letter to arrive from the States at that time. Bobbie Bosse, Patti's sister, had written a letter to us with a "p.s." which simply read, "Don't know why but I felt God wanted me to include this check." We received that letter the Monday after helping the pastor's family. It just proved to us again, that when God speaks and His people respond, He then blesses us with just what we need. Thank you Lord! Three weeks before is nothing to Him!

The next project that we got involved in was we visited Frank Howell and his family in Cagayan de Oro City. They were Bible Baptist Missionaries. We had met them during our first term on the field. Frank Howell, the Bible Baptist Missionary was a good friend of ours, and he had started a local Bible School. He was in need of teachers. There was another American missionary family there. The Robinson's, and were also interested in teaching. We all met at the Bible Baptist Church with the pastor, and we began to plan the courses, and who was to teach what. I was greatly interested in this particular work since the Bible School we had used in the past, up in the mountains was not as proper of doctrine as I would have liked it to be. It happened to be more of the Baptist doctrine we were used to. Central Missionary Clearinghouse (our mission) was of the same doctrine. It so happened that not only was I accepted in with them but, I would teach Genesis, Revelation, Hebrews and Preachers & Preaching Methodology, Patti taught English and Health. This was a great endeavor! Both of the other missionaries, and Patti and I, would begin to bring all our new students there for their Bible training. This worked out great.

Another one of my jobs was going with some of the pastors up into the mountains and doing revival meetings, since I knew how to preach some in the Cebuano dialect. That was exciting, as we would sometimes be gone a week at a time. There was such a thirst for the

Bible in those days of the 1980's. I can remember that after the evening meeting, about 9:00 p.m., the people would be sitting around and just asking question after question, growing in the knowledge of the Word of God.

We had to go up to Manila where our children were going to school. Patsy was graduating from high school that year. We also had to go to the Marcos' Theatre, one of the evening's, as Patsy, was in a big musical called "The Music Man." I remember that she did a remarkable job. It was great! The day after she graduated, our family spent a day in the city of Manila, shopping and having a good time with Patsy before she headed back to the States. In fact, as I recall, she left the following day. Her plane flew to California, and then to New York, then she had a limousine ride to Newark, New Jersey. Her aunt, Bobbie (Patti's sister) picked her up from there. It was not easy for us to see her off without us, but she traveled with a group from Faith Academy. She planned to be at Liberty Baptist Bible College that August. That would make us both feel a lot better about her. We brought the other children down to Mindanao Island with us for that summer. We had a great time and they received a bit of education on church-planting ministries. They also met the Howell children, and the Robinson children.

After the kids went back to school that fall, we had the opportunity to go to a tiny Island off Mindanao Island, called Camigan Island. There were two small churches on that Island. Each one had a pastor. The problem was that there were only a few worshippers in each of those two churches. We offered our help and they accepted it. What that meant was that I would go over there with one of our local pastors and do revival meetings. We would begin to teach them the teacher Training Courses. This would help develop them into good sound Bible teachers. It created an extra work for us. We now had Gingoog Baptist Church, Side 7 Bible center, Side 2 Bible center, the church where Alice and her husband were, a college Bible study, and a teen Bible study. We were also teaching in the Bible College doing revival meetings, and now helping with these two churches. I remember saying to Patti, "I'll be very happy when we have some more trained pastors."

Thank the Lord for answered prayer! A pastor from the Doan Baptist Bible College, on another Island to the north, came to help in the work on Camigan Island. This meant that we now had a total of four churches and two Bible centers.

It was evident at that time that we must band together as a group. We had a meeting with the pastors and Bible women, plus some of the city officials. The result of that meeting meant that we were able to incorporate into ""The Coastline Fellowship of Baptist Churches of Northern Mindanao Island." I must say that we were very happy!

The children had come back down to our Island from school for their summer break. I began bringing our son Troy with me on some of the outreaches. One particular day, we had planned to go to a new outreach up in the Mountain. Troy did not realize what that trip involved at the time. I had an old '52 MacArthur Jeep. I had a complete waterproof kit on the motor. I also had the exhaust pipe fitted so it went up through the back of the front fender and up about 5'. All of this was work was done so that I could go through the small streams, and the motor would not quit. As long as you kept the motor running, that is! We were going down into the stream when I looked over and he was reaching straight out with his hand patting the mud and water smiling! What a boy! He was enjoying every bit of it until he was sitting there with water over his knees. He soon discovered like the rest of us that with the heat and humidity, you could get wet one minute, and dry the next!

Another time that Troy wanted to go with me was on a new outreach that I just had heard of. A relative of one of our national church leaders invited me to go up into the mountain to a place called Tumpagoon, on the Davao side of the mountain.

It was a lot farther than any of our other places of outreach. It also, was an area mixed with many Muslim people. Troy and I were told, that we needed go to the market place in Gingoog where we lived, and be there by 4:30 a.m. We were to catch the logging truck. These trucks were the only vehicles allowed up in that area. It was a big logging sector and they had all rights to the road. That way the logging trucks as they came down the mountain would not have an accident with another vehicle. We managed to catch the logging truck that morning, and found many other people that got on the truck. It was a very rough ride and you held on for dear life at times! I remember along the way the truck stopped at one point because there were people in the road all excited! They had killed a wild boar and were selling chunks of the meat. The truck drive and others bought some of it, which they cooked when we arrived at our destination. I can still recall Troy, as he tasted the wild boar. It really surprised him because it actually was very tasty. There was a certain girl there in the village that caught his attention. I noticed them taking a quick glance at each other. It stopped fast when she opened her mouth with a great big smile and her teeth were all red from chewing Betel Nut. This particular nut has a drug chemical, which causes you to be addicted to it. I was glad to have had my son with me those days up in the mountain. It gave him a bit of what the mission field was all about. However, the children had to go back to Manila for school.

Ling, and her sister Pat, had now graduated from Bible College and decided to join in our endeavors for the Lord. Pat became engaged to a young man who was a pastor. They took over one of the struggling churches in Camigan Island. That meant, both of those churches now had pastors. Ling wanted to live in a small barrio just a few kilometers from us, called Medina. She had a desire to just live there and be a witness for Jesus her Lord, like "Mom and Sir Pierce." We helped her setup house keeping and in three weeks time she had two new believers! After about three months, she started holding religious classes in the public school and had a small group coming to her home for Bible study. God opened a new work there through her. It was not long before she met and finally married, a young man who had been trained to be a pastor. It was at this time, (in 1985) that we felt God would have us go on furlough again. Troy was to graduate that year and we were to be up there in Manila for his graduation. I also was developing what Patti thought was a heart problem. So we packed up, and put our belongings in storage. We also spent a few days with the Robinson family and the

Howell family before leaving on furlough.

When we arrived in Manila, we found out that Troy was to be in a musical called, "Brigadoon." I remember that he and his "buddy" Brian Beverly became a couple of "hams" on stage! The Beverly family, were from Davao City and served with another Baptist mission board. We spent a day shopping for trinkets to bring back to the States and got our Visas ready to depart that following evening at 5:00p.m! So off we flew, to the United States for our second furlough.

Jesus made a statement, "I am the Bread of life."

As a Christian, how much of an importance do we put on that Bread we hold (The Bible) in relationship to others? Can we see "the fields white unto harvest?" The sight of the fields reveals our duty because as the apostle Paul says, "We are debtors to the gospel of Jesus Christ."

15

OUT OF THE ASHES!

We arrived in California and were picked up at the airport and taken to Fellowship Crating and Missionary services. We spent a week there getting over Jet lag and becoming "Americanized"… once again!

The following day Mr. Hendricks gave us a tour of the warehouse where many things were done for missionaries from all over the world. Not only did they crate up items that different missionaries took to the field, but they also had personal hygiene items that companies donated for the missionaries as well. Occasionally a missionary left a vehicle there for them to sell. That particular day there was an Oldsmobile wagon that a missionary had left. They wished to sell the wagon to another missionary. We are a missionary family in need of a vehicle. It was just the right price for us. It was in real good shape, so we bought it to drive across the United States. Troy, our oldest son had just graduated from School, and we had planned to spend some good quality time with him sight-seeing!

We left California and spent two days at the Grand Canyon. That was absolutely, beautiful! We all loved it, especially the sunsets. We even have pictures of our adopted son, Jason, with a little cowboy hat and boots on, standing on the rim of the canyon! We left there, and headed toward Tyler, Texas to our mission office (Central Missionary Clearinghouse). As we were driving, we came upon the Hopi Indian reservation, where we toured the rock caves and places of interest that were there. It certainly opened our eyes! On the way to Texas, out in the middle of no-where, we happened upon this huge crater. A meteor had landed years ago, and it was now an official tourist attraction. They took us by elevator, down 8 floors to the bottom. This must have been some meteor! Upon arriving in Texas, we realized just how big that state was, from the north to the south! We saw all the wide-open places, tumbleweed, oil fields, and cattle. The road seemed to go on straight as far as the eye could see! We spent a few days with Joel and Chris Harris our friends from our home church in Greene, New York. Our goal was to get to Pasadena and Tyler, Texas. These were suburbs of Houston, where our mission office was located. The mission office and church had different addresses. The mission office driveway was on a different address line than the church. Brother Jack Bridge was the president of the mission. Our family had a great time there, and spent the night before heading to our next destination: Jacksonville, Florida.

I do not know if any of you have ever been across U.S. Route # 10, from Texas to Florida, but most of the way across Louisiana, is bayou… country-swamp! It is a long way for children not to be able to see anything but cement barriers. Once we arrived in Florida, the rest of the trip to Bradenton was nice.

We spent a week at the D & D Missionary homes. All the houses were set up for missionaries, and are not only furnished, but completely stocked with food as well. The only requirement from us was to give a few hours of labor a week. I mowed lawns for two days, and Patti worked a few hours in their clothing room. Our entire family was fully fitted with clothes from this room, and all free! They were beautiful homes. The Jennings family, were friends from New York and were also there. We all went sight- seeing and swimming together.

Our next stop was in Lynchburg, Virginia. Patsy, if you remember, had graduated and come home from the Philippines ahead of us, had gone here to college. She was one of three girls that rented a room together. One of the girls was Angel Fekete. She had a brother by the name of David Fekete, and I'm not sure all that transpired, but Patsy ended up getting married to him! He did come to the Philippines with Patsy to get our blessing before the marriage though. We had a good time with them! Troy was also interested in checking out the Liberty Baptist College where he ended up going that fall.

As you can tell by now, it took quite a while before we made it home to New York. We did finally arrive there and spent three weeks with family and friends in the Madison and the North Brookfield area. However, we were ready to put down stakes! After a few telephone calls and other events, it was very evident that we were to be in the area of Greene, New York. This was so that we could be in our sending church and the children could attend Central Baptist Academy. They were used to that school and the students.

We located a nice farmhouse on Sapbush Road. It was located next to the Conover family. They were one of the families from our church. One of the other families from the church had a big barn filled with furniture. He was a retired military man that had accumulated the furnishings. He told us that the Lord had given him the furnishings, and he felt the Lord wanted him to share them. This was a blessing and we had all we needed to set up house keeping. We gave our Oldsmobile wagon to a family who were going to Bible College, and they gave us their old Chevy, which Patti drove for local use. I was able to go to Jonestown, Pa. where they have cars for missionaries to use while on deputation. The only fee was for the insurance cost. This was a big help for many missionaries and I drove away with a Subaru wagon.

We then started our deputation and reporting to our sending churches. There were 300 prayer warriors and 37 churches to contact. Patti and I also worked on Wednesday evenings in the A.W.A.N.A. program at church. Then came the Mission conferences and banquets. It was a busy, busy year! We had lost support from two of the churches for various reasons, yet God provided in other ways. We had some very nice meetings in our supporting churches and one new church began to support us. All was going well, yet I personally did not feel that well. I did not tell any one at the time about my health, and just kept going.

As the winter was coming fast that year in New York, I needed to get much wood stored. The wood stove was what we used for heat. There was also a lot snow in New York. I needed to get snow tires for the car. (You definitely needed them back in those days)! We also had to get winter clothes! I look back and wonder why we ever lived up in the North, yet I know God had us where He wanted us to be.

Patsy, David, and Troy used to come home from Lynchburg to see us at different times. We would all wait up and surprise them with soda and pizza from Pudgies Pizza. That was always a treat for the whole family! It seemed as though it did not take much to please them back in those days. Even the little things like going up in the woods and cutting our down own Christmas tree was entertaining. They all had fun with simple little things.

That following spring was an adventure that we will never forget! On one particular Monday in March, Patti, Ling (who we brought to America with us) and I went up to West Eaton, New York to see a professional beautician. She was a member of the church there. She had offered to do Mom and Ling's hair when they came. We had decided to get Ling's hair done before she flew back to the Philippines. However, upon arriving there, she was not home. We did not have any other reason for going, so decided to come back home, have lunch, and take a nap. As we came down the knoll approaching the house, we noticed fire trucks and many people at our home. The house had caught on fire, destroying much of the main structure. The firemen that worked the scene had already shoved the wall inward where my office was. It happened to be the only wall, which had not completely burned. It only had some water damage. This was a major concern to me because all our slides that we used for deputation were there, plus our Philippine items. Our Visa's and Passports were there as well. Praise God they were all intact! The Red Cross offered to give us housing, but we waited for a while to get our thoughts together. Pastor Rogers came and prayed with us plus gave us some council. Then one of the deacons from the church called the Conover family where we were. He said, "I just put an ad in the local paper that my apartment was for rent. I just called now and cancelled the ad because I would like your family to live in it for the last four months of your furlough." WOW! God's time is always perfect.

The following day we went over to the house that burned and searched around to see what was worth saving. After moving some of the debris where the office had been, I found the slides were under the steel desk and had not even had water damage. I also found the briefcase with the Passports and Visa's. It was good to see that it was free from any damage. God sure put His hand on all that He knew we needed. We were not able to save much else. The Red Cross met with Patti and me the next day. They gave us vouchers for Burn's Furniture Warehouse where we were able to get all our furniture replaced. The Red Cross gave us some vouchers to go to K-mart, where we received three complete outfits of clothing each. Many of the area churches brought us different items that we needed. We never ever experienced anything like it before. For the first time in years, we now had new furniture, new clothes, and so much more than we expected. We serve an awesome God!

Three weeks later, on Easter Sunday, when we were on our way to Morrisville Baptist Church, the motor in our car started knocking. We were able to make it there and were parking the car when it died! It was hard for me to preach that Sunday morning. Patti's sister Nancy, including her family was also there at the church. After the service that morning, we went with them to their house, and then Nancy took us back down to our home in Greene, New York. We had lost a house with all of the contents plus a car, all in one month's time.

That following week, one of the deacons let me borrow their car to look for a vehicle of our own. I found a Plymouth Valiant that we could afford. We bought it for $ 400.00, {do not laugh. Cars were much cheaper then}! We drove that car for the rest of our meetings.

Remember me telling of the furniture that one of the church members had given to us? It had burned in the fire! God took the furniture in that fire, and gave that family back new furniture. Is not God great? They thought we should keep it. But, we had no use for it since we were going back to the Philippines. God also had another surprise for us! We still needed to raise money for our return tickets to the Philippines. God provided again! The owner of the house where we had the fire received his check from the insurance company. The tithe that he gave to us was the exact amount we needed for our tickets! It came the week we were to leave. There was much excitement in the home church as God moved one step at a time! We called the travel agent in Virginia, and told us to pick up the tickets on our way to Florida.

We bought a car carrier and put it on the top of the Plymouth, filled it with our suitcases and proceeded on our way. We stopped at the Christian Travel Agency, picked up our tickets, and got our Passports and Visa's all ready. We then went to see our daughter, Patsy, and her husband David. We spent three days there with them and then left for Florida. There were two reasons for going to Florida. One was that our pastor wanted us to have a two- week rest. The other reason was that Florida in July is like the Philippines. This allowed us to become ac-climated to the hot humid weather.

We had a great family time! We visited many of the theme parks and water fun places. Soon we would be back in the Philippines. Our daughters, Carla and Kandi would be staying at Faith Academy while Jason would be with us on Mindanao Island where Mom would home school him for a year before he entered the local Filipino School. This was the fall of 1986, and we were heading back to the Philippine Islands.

16

A BIG CHANGE IN MINISTRY!

We went back into the mountain outreaches to visit, but noticed a lot of military activity all around us. The Philippine Army and the rebels were engaged in many fights not just here but on many of the Islands. It was hard at times for us to tell the difference between them because the rebels would wear parts of uniforms that they had stolen from the soldiers. However, whoever flagged you down for a ride, you asked no questions, you had to let them climb on, and then continued on your way. It was also very difficult for the mountain people. The Philippine army took much of their produce and livestock, as well as some of their young women. The rebels would not only use their supplies but they would try to indoctrinate them into ideals that were not common to their way of thinking, such as Communism and Islamic teaching.

I had gone over to the People's Palace to take care of some government business for the churches, where I met the mayor. He invited me into his office for a visit. He then let me know that his government workers were well informed as to our outreach work in the mountains. He thanked me for helping his people. He then went on to let me know that many of the leaders from the rural outreaches worked in his offices. Because of the fact that we as missionaries could be in a crossfire situation and be hurt or killed in our travels up in the mountains, it would be better if we stopped going up there. He had a big conference hall up stairs in the People's Palace, and he wanted me to come each Friday at 2:00 p.m. and do my Bible teaching there. That Bible study would be to all the village leaders! I would teach them, and then have them in turn teach their own people!

Since the rebel situation was a becoming a major problem, it was clear to us that Gingoog City seemed to be a very troubled spot. This meant that being an American and living there would not be a good thing. We then looked at housing all along the coastline, where we could continue teaching in the Bible Institute with Frank Howell, but we could go back to Gingoog City and teach in the People's Palace. We had transportation again now since I had purchased Frank's Honda 750 motorcycle. The Lord led us to a village just outside Cagayan De Oro City. We could continue doing all our previous work, and start a new ministry with the fishing village. This was right on the bay, where we heard the waves, and felt the breeze. It was a bit different from where we had lived previously.

Brother Howell and his family went home that year on furlough. That only left Brother John Robinson, Patti, and I, to teach at the Bible Seminary. However, what I did not know was that Frank had trained the local pastor, Pastor Jualie, to teach two of his classes.

This local pastor and I immediately hit it off. He liked the fact that I could speak some Cebuano. It was not long until he had me going on different trips with him doing "open air meetings." The busy schedule at that time was quite heavy. I did not realize at that time how it was effecting, my heart.

That March, Patti & I went back up to Manila, to Faith Academy to see Carla & Kandi. Jason stayed at home with one of the students from the Bible School where we taught. We arrived at Faith Academy and had a good time with the girls. The following evening, we went to see Carla in a musical production. She did a great job! The following night was her graduation, and our plan was to spend the day in Manila, shopping with the girls before we were to head back home. We found some stores that sold U.S. dry goods. It was nice to be able to buy a U.S. candy bar. I remember that I had bought a Butterfinger bar, and when I tasted it, it tasted like Tide Soap! Apparently, when they had bought all the items, they threw it in one box all together, and the soap of course, overpowered everything else! It had not been a good buy!

That summer, Patti, Carla, Kandi, Jason and I were finally a family once again which was nice. We had picnics on our shelter by the sea. We could swim everyday and enjoy the beach. It was not long before Kandi had decided not to go back to Faith Academy since Carla had graduated. This meant that we had to look into some schooling options for Kandi. We found out about a local Chinese high school where the Howell's daughter went. So, Kandi went to school there, and Jason went there as well. He really liked it! Maybe it was freedom from his mother. This gave Patti time to teach and help the young women from the Bible Baptist Church and the Bible school where we taught. She enjoyed a chance to work in the ministry, and all the women seemed to like her as well. (Of course, I could not think of anybody not liking Patti).

That fall was especially interesting and hard for Patti & me. One evening we had heard a thud and wondered what the noise could have been. It so happened that Jason had been climbing on the cabinets and closets in his room. He had got almost to the top (about six feet) and fell. When we went and discovered him, he was trying to stand up. He was dizzy, and disoriented. He told us his head hurt, and we could see blood oozing a bit from his ear. Patti took him to the walk-in shower for some cold water, tried to keep him awake and quiet. The problem that we had was that he needed to go to the hospital fast to get checked out. We did not have any transportation at the time but our motorcycle. We knew that the teen meeting Carla & Kandi had gone to should be finished. That meant they would be returning on the jeep that the young people had. We tried to keep Jason calm, but by this time, he was vomiting blood. After the Jeep arrived we all took Jason to the hospital. He was immediately, admitted! We soon learned that he had a concussion, and a hairline fracture of his skull behind the ear! We spent a total of five days with him in the hospital. God was so good to us! When we look back at that incident, knowing he landed on a concrete floor from 6 feet up, it scares us to think what could have happened.

After the Bible School let out for the summer, I was able to spend more time with the Coastline Fellowship Churches. The work was a bit different, in that I was doing in-depth studies with the pastors and workers of those churches, teaching them to teach and to train their own leaders. The Friday Bible studies were still going on in the People's Palace, and we also, had a new Bible study group in the Barrio (village) where we lived. These people had no idea that someone really loved them. They were outcasts and had just about nothing. They did not have gardens or fruit trees, or crops of any kind. These families were fishing people and if they caught no fish, they had nothing!

Occasionally I would leave these works for one week or more and go with Pastor Juale for revival meetings. I remember one particular time we were hiking up into an area and some nationals were coming from the opposite direction. There were two men from the area with Pastor and I. I noticed that they began to surround me and they told me to be quiet. I had noticed a female in the oncoming group that looked very nice, yet a bit peculiar! After the party had passed, the two men, that knew the area, told us that the woman was a "witch." They told me that if she could get close to me, she would have scratched me with her fingernail that had poison under the nail. A witch was fond of poisoning someone, and taking advantage of them robbing them. I was sure glad these men were with us that day! It just proves to us that when we ask God's protection over the day, He gives it! I always enjoyed my time working side by side with these national brothers.

Another time we were up on an Island north of Mindanao. We had gone to Cebu Island by boat the night before, and took a bus to the ferry, which would take us to our destination. We were met by some of the people there, and enjoyed our time with them. The third night we were there, we heard a lot of noise during the night. Many of the men had gone outside, I did not know why, but the following morning when we woke up, Pastor told me to pack my things because we were leaving. It was on our way home that the men shared with me that rebels had found out what we were doing, and that they had an American with them. They knew that the rebels would be there that next night and only God would know what would have happened.

One of the neat things of these revival meetings was to see people coming from great distances to the services, hiking for kilometer after kilometer. They would pack a place out with people. After the meeting, they would stay for an hour or two and would ask us Bible questions. They seemed so eager to learn! Then, they would hike back home, rise early, work all day, and hike back to church repeating this all week.

Our third year back there would prove to be different yet. There were more national pastors trained, and they began to take more of the responsibility. The Apostle Paul had been my great example in the ministry. He would train, then after three years or so, he moved on. It became clear to us that the Coastline Fellowship of Baptist Churches was doing great. The nationals were taking much more of the work load that we had been involved with. I had not let anybody know, but my health had been deteriorating. I was not feeling as well as I should. I did not know what it was, I only knew that my chest was tight most of the time and I was so tired.

My plan at that time was to keep training the nationals to take over the work. I had begun to back out of some ministries, letting them do more of the work that they had been trained to do. I continued to teach in the Bible School. However, some of the national pastors also taught as well. I also spoke in many of the churches, encouraging them in the work. Our home had become a training center as well. Many came and spent two days or a week at a time learning all they could. Patti and I began to give them our books from my library; many of teaching tools; our portable organ; white boards; and children's Bible story, books. I had to decide who was to receive many of my study and research materials. Yes, we were heading home to the States that April for a furlough and a health work up; and for rest. If we were to come back to the Philippines, it would be to a whole new area, since the work here was going along on its own now. Like Paul, our work here had come to an end and it was time for them to walk in the faith.

We gave away much of our furnishings, sold some of the main

items, packed up barrels with personal items, and got our shipping labels for the barrels. We then got our Visas and Passports in order, sold our car and our motorcycle, and bought our tickets to the U.S.A.

We again landed in California at Fellowship Crating and Missionary Services. We actually went to the same motel with the kitchenette that we had stayed in the previous furlough. While we were there, we learned that Frank Howell, with his family would be arriving that same week after finishing family furlough in the United States. Jason and our two girls were excited to get to see them again. They were heading back to the Philippines so we waited for a couple of days to see them. When they arrived we all had fun! The two families again! Both Frank and I decided to take our families to the local Theme Park the next day. Boy was that a blast! Especially since his family and ours both had two girls and one boy each. We had a good time sharing and going over the ministries back in the Philippines. Everybody had a great time together.

Frank was driving a real nice Toyota mini motor home with a tag axle underneath the rear because of its length. It was large for being a mini motor home. He asked me if I could sell it for him when I arrived in New York. The next morning I called two different banks and discovered that he wanted far less than what the value of it was. I told him that we could sell it and send his money to him when we arrived in New York. Frank handed the keys to us and we put our own insurance on it, and packed our things into it. Patti and I figured that if his family had been comfortable in it, then we could as well since our family was the same size. Frank also had a large carrier that he had put on the top. We were able to put some of the extra luggage in that.

Wow! Here we were back in the States, driving across the U.S. in a mini motor home. What an awesome God we serve! It was a bit funny to hear different people talk about that little motor home, when we were at different campsites. I would ask folks about their gas mileage on their bigger motor homes, and then tell them we got 14-15 miles per gallon! We knew it would take us a few days to get to Michigan where Patsy and her family lived. We spent some time site seeing along the way.

We spent a week with Patsy and her family. She had a cute little house. Patti and I were glad to see our first grandchild. A cute little boy!

I remember thinking that I was not that old yet! Patsy and her husband Dave were very busy in their local church. They liked the fact that we were now home in the States again. Naturally, it is hard being so far from your children and not able to hug or kiss them occasionally. We were in Michigan with them about ten days.

It was while we were there with them that Pastor Tom Ross from Faith Baptist church in Morrisville, New York called me and asked me a question I had never been asked, before. The question leads into the next chapter.
"

God will use us, if we are willing to be used!

17

WHAT ARE YOU TEACHING US LORD?

The big question from Pastor Tom Ross was if Patti and I would be willing to work in their Church/School at Faith Baptist Church in Morrisville, New York. This was the church that we helped going door-to-door evangelism just before heading to the mission field. They had been meeting in the Agricultural building. God had blessed and their church became a reality. Therefore, Patti and I were familiar with the work there. They also supported the work in the Philippines. So, we said good bye to Patsy and her family and headed out to New York.

We arrived in New York, and spent time with Patti's folks, and my family. We knew that God was doing some changing in our lives. However, what did the future hold for us? God never makes a mistake. I am sure by now that you know He closes one door and opens another for us. We then decided to make a time to meet with pastor Ross and the board from the school / church and see if God was giving us a different door of ministry for us. It turned out that the meeting was only with the pastor. He told us that they wanted me to be the Principal/ Administrator and Patti a teacher. They also sent me to the satellite school of the School of Tomorrow. It was to be held in lower part of the state of Michigan. Patti and I did accept the job, and had decided that

Patti; Jason; Carla; and Kandi would stay at Patsy's, in upper Michigan, (which they did not mind at all), while I went to the school. It was a crash course, which consisted of six long tiring days. I remember the time well. I did pass the course, and went up to Patsy's, spent three days there before we all headed back to New York.

One of the families from the Faith Baptist Church, where the Christian School was, gave us a Ford wagon to drive, so that we did not have to go all around in the motor home. They also had an apartment, which at that time was available. God was at work. We had a car and now an apartment on North Street in Morrisville, New York. However, we did not live there very long since it was quite small. One of the farmers that we knew in the area had sold his cows and was heading to Bible School. He wanted someone to move into the farmhouse and rent it. We decided to do this since we loved the out doors, the farmhouse and with all the room for the kids to run around, it was perfect for young Jason, our son. It was during the time we were there that Troy brought his wife-to-be home for us to meet. We thought she was nice right from day one! About three weeks later, we invited her parents to come for dinner on the farm. We all had a very good time. They were from Cortland Baptist Church and very nice people.

Another surprise was that many of the people from the church in Morrisville and West Eaton Baptist church, had given us used furniture as well. God had supplied all our needs. We seemed to be very blessed of God! God had another blessing at that time. The pastor had a paper route that he did each morning, Monday through Friday. He asked me if I would be a substitute route driver for him, and I told him I would. It was a newspaper route, which supplied many of the convenience stores and grocery markets. In other words, they were places that took anywhere from 25-50 papers each. I knew at the time, it would help supply our needs during the summer months before the school started. We soon became members of the church. My personal conviction is that if you are associated in any way with a church, then you need to be a member of that church. The reason for this is so that everyone is of the same thinking in all areas of what you and the board are doing.

School was underway and this meant that each Sunday evening after the service, we had to set up the tables and set up the learning centers. On each Friday, we took it all back down, and set up the sanctuary for Sunday services.

The students were not only children of the church members, but also some who were not. This was a good tool of outreach in the community. Most of the children really liked and wanted to be there in the school. However, we did have two students that were not "happy campers" there. This created some interesting meetings with the board. It also was during that time, the pastor resigned his position and the board began to let me know very plainly, that they did not even want the school to function that school year. However, we would all get through the year and close it next summer. It is interesting how God sets things all in motion and man gets in the way and tears it down. Oh well, to God be the glory! We finished the job that Pastor Ross had called us to do that year. Patti had a good time with her students as well. We had two graduate that year one was our own daughter, Kandi. That summer they did close the school and we did not have a job! I know that just as God closed this door, He has another open for me.

The other student that graduated from the Christian school was from a different church. I met the pastor from his church at his graduation party. It was my first time to meet his pastor and it appeared that he wanted to talk with me. I remember we had gone outside when he shared with me that he knew about the closure of the school. He told me that his church also had a school and that he was looking for help. He would like me to come and be the Principal/Administrator for their school. That summer, Patti and I met with him at his church and we told him we would help him that year. The curriculum would allow some teaching as well on my part. Patti would teach English for the whole school, plus health. It would prove to be an exciting year! We were doing quite well and had bought a mobile home in Sherburne, New York. This way our money was going into something of our own.

About that same time, Carla had an accident with the Ford wagon which totaled it. Troy and Kandi were with her when it happened. I was glad that it was the full size wagon, other wise they, would have been hurt very badly. God had protected our family! Patti and I had a Volkswagen Quantum, (made by Audi), with a five-cylinder engine.

The Bible Baptist Christian School had started for the year and all was going well. We were comfortable in our mobile home and had met some of the new neighbors. Jason helped one neighbor with odd jobs and was having a good time. However, something was in the air that we did not anticipate coming!

It was now November of 1989. I still had not been feeling well again. I thought at the time that it was probably just a chest cold. I had a part time job at a local Grand Union super market in Norwich, New York. (If you recall dear reader, I had cut meat for Grand Union before my Bible School days). My job was to run the Deli and keep the meat counter full of meat three evenings a week. It was so much easier now days since the meat all came in boxes. (The meat used to come, hanging on rails. Whole sides that you balanced on your shoulder and prayed it did not fall to the ground!!) I had worked there for about three weeks. It used to be very busy on Friday nights. It seemed like everybody wanted sliced meats and cheese. They also wanted subs, which we sold as well. That particular Friday night the line was long. I would have them leave pieces of paper with their name, what they wanted, and how much. The line seemed especially long that night! I remember that I was about halfway through the customer list, when I just felt very tired, and weak. I apparently fell to the floor, because that is where I was when I came to. The store manager told me that I did not look very well and that I should go home.

I drove home and went to bed. The car was one Troy had and I only had driven it to work. I do not remember how I got home! Patti was out at a meeting and when she came home, she wanted to know why I was home so early. I told her I did not feel well. She called the V.A. hospital in Syracuse, New York. They wanted me to come in right away, but since it was an hour or more drive, I told Patti I would go in the morning, and I did. When we arrived the following day, they admitted me and told me that I definitely had some heart complications. I remember that I was there two days and they did a stress test. The third day they did a heart cauterization, and discovered I had two blocked arteries. I was there a few more days before they told me that I would have to go to Buffalo, New York for my heart Angioplasty. They would have liked for me to go right then, but Thanksgiving was that week! I told them that I had two speaking engagements and two Thanksgiving meetings that I was scheduled to be at. It was decided at the time, that I would arrive in Buffalo, New York on December the 8th.

Patti, Carla and I went to Buffalo, New York the morning of the 8th. They checked me out from head to toe and told me that the procedure they would do was just a bit risky! What they told us was that usually there would not be any complications. However, the chances of complications were about 30%. Well, the next day, while in the procedure room, I remember watching the monitor and feeling them push the wire up in the vessel. I watched as it came to the first vessel, there was pressure in my chest and all went ok. Wow! I thought this was not bad at all. The next one was very different. I remember watching the screen. All of a sudden, I thought my chest would explode, and something cold on my leg! Later I found out that the plaque inside the artery in the heart had crystallized and hardened, so when they pulled the balloon it ruptured! I had to have an emergency bypass!

The next thing I had remembered was Patti and Carla telling someone that they were going for coffee. Now wait a minute! They promised me coffee after the procedure, even if it went in the I.V.! I had not realized that I could not talk, something was in my throat, I was in a strange room, and I was feeling very, very sore. They did tell me later that the nurse caught me writing with my finger on the sheet, a big "C". I apparently wanted some coffee badly. They took me up to my room from recovery later that day. There in the room I saw balloons, and there was a birthday card, that played "Happy Birthday." It was December 9th, my birthday!! Wow!

The following week I spent in bed. However, they did get me up occasionally to walk around the room. My pain was never sharp. It seemed like I was sort of kicked by a horse in the chest. It was a dull aching pain. I do remember the day they came in to take the staples out of me. From the top of my chest, to my mid-section, and then from the top of my thigh, to my ankle were these staples. They told me that it would not hurt as they took them out. I remember well all those staples coming out. Each one stung and hurt! However, the following days I began to walk a bit more, and it was easier since the staples were out. That next week I came home. Now, the 7 months recuperation began. (I understand that the whole procedure now days, is a small slit and three weeks recovery).

During my recovery time, I went to Colgate College, which was nearby, and walked five days a week. It was only a few days before that the pastor from the Christian school where I worked came and told me he did not need my services anymore! Talk about kicking someone when they are down!?! He also began to harass Patti to the point that she quit! I remember that God supplied our needs all through that time in ways beyond our comprehension. Praise His Holy Name! (God was telling us not to put down tent pegs!)

Patti & I had been attending Faith Baptist church in Sherburne, New York, and doing a little visitation for Pastor Carpenter. We liked the little church and the people there. One thing we did while we were there was to take one of their Missionary families to Michigan. They had come home for furlough, and needed to get to Michigan. Since we had two cars at that time, we let them drive one and we followed. Then we visited our daughter and son in law, after which, Patti drove one car while I drove the other back home. It had felt good to help a fellow missionary.

When we arrived back home, we discovered that Pastor Carpenter and his wife were very sick. Patti & I went tried to go over to their house every day. Patti would make some soup, and they would try to eat. We did as much of his visitation as we could for him, and did whatever else we could do. He had at the time already taken the position of Pastor at Cortland Baptist, but had to get well before he could move.

One day while I was with him, he shared with me that he knew of a pastor friend of his from Practical Bible Training School that needed a Principal /Administrator. He then called the Pastor and had me talk to him. Pastor Caldwell asked if I would come and meet with him. My health had been improving, so I did just that. I arrived in Wellsboro, Pa. the following Monday. Pastor Caldwell was a young eager and energetic man that had a desire to share Christ with anyone he met. The church/school building was new, with lots of room for growth. I remember thinking at the time that it had some real potential!

We moved our mobile home down there that summer, up into the woods. I remember that Jason loved it. We had settled in, Patti had her room at the school ready, and I had the office in order. The A. C. E. curriculum had come in, plus, we had new students that had registered, we were ready. One of the first things that I wanted to do was to meet with all the teachers and get to know them. This way we would all know what the program would be and how to address and solve problems that would come up.

The school was actually going very well! Pastor Caldwell and I were very pleased. We even had new students come and more that were interested. I remember one evening, Pastor wanted me to take his Colony Park Mercury wagon and take some teens to a Word of Life rally. However, I already had committed myself to another meeting and could not go for him. On the way home from that meeting, a drunk driver hit the pastor's wagon instantly killing him, three of his children, and the two drunk drivers. Jason, our son, was in the back of the wagon and received a fractured right hip. The accident was bad enough at the time, however, what happened next really hit Patti & I hard.

The pastor's wife began to tell every body that I should have been the one killed, not her husband. Two deacons also were caught up in the emotional stress! I immediately sought counsel from another Pastor that I knew there in Wellsboro, Pa., who also had a child in the school and knew all about what was happening. He told me that in many situations like this, there had to be a "scapegoat" I had thus become the scapegoat! What they wanted was to have Patti and I leave the school and church. In their thinking, this would remedy the whole thing. I then had called a meeting with the board of the school. We first met with the pastor that I had received counsel from. The outcome of that meeting was not good. The school board had made up their mind that I was to go. I told them that I had made a commitment to Pastor Caldwell. The commitment was that I would stay for at least one year. They allowed me to finish out the school year.

Folks, I don't know about you but the question that came to me was, what does God want with me?? I could not go back to the Philippines because of my heart condition. I had at that time been in three difficult Christian school experiences, now "what, Lord?"

I remember telling you back a few chapters that I had told the Lord, "anything but a pastor, Lord!" Well, guess what....

18

ARE YOU SURE LORD A PASTOR?

If you recall, I had made a statement while I was in Bible College, that I would do anything for the Lord but be a pastor. I had seen how deacon boards and people who think it is their church and not God's, try to run the church instead of letting the pastor (under shepherd) lead the flock that God called him to lead. I thought I had seen it all. We had spent ten years in the Philippines as missionaries, and could not go back to that work because of my heart condition. In Mindanao,, it was too far from any good health facilities back then. My medical help was only Veterans Administration. We had stayed in the States and had spent three years in Christian School education. God had shut the first one down because they actually did not want a Christian school. The second Christian school was when I had my open-heart surgery and the pastor told me he did not need my services anymore. Then the third year was the accident where the pastor and some of his children were killed. To those at that church, it became clear that "I" was the fault. They needed what appeared to be a "scapegoat", me! The deacon board allowed me to finish that year because of a promise I had made to the pastor who.

A good Christian friend of mine, who had traveled with his family, singing & preaching, told me about a church up in western New York that was in need of a pastor. I still wanted to serve God in some way for sure, and I had needed some sort of income to support my family. That is no reason to go into a pastorate. Pastors usually do not get rich! We had been in the ministry long enough to know that God will not give a call to His work but what He has all the details worked out. If I was to be a pastor, He already knew how I felt and He would see to it that by His sustaining grace I would be able to do the work, even if it were to be a pastor. After we had been praying about it for a week, Patti and I decided to write to that church and give them my credentials, and see if they contacted me back. We knew God would either open or shut the door.

It was just about a week's time and they gave us a date to come and preach. I believe that it was in June of 1990 that we went there. Patti and I sang, gave testimony, and I preached both in the morning and the evening services. We had gone back home and not thought much about it again until one day a formal letter came from them with their doctrinal statement enclosed, to see if we were in agreement with them in practice and doctrine. They informed me that they were pleased with us in what they saw while we were previously with them, and we were to come back as soon as we could as candidates for pastor and wife. Two weeks later we did just that! We had a great time there with them. The following week, they let me know that I was to become their pastor, and that I was to start the first Sunday of August. We moved there the last week of July, and I was going to learn fast what a pastorate is. I soon realized that all my years in the ministry up to that point had been preparing me for the new work that God had laid ahead.

The church began to grow in number in fact almost doubled, and we had started two home Bible studies. We had a bus at the time, and had begun to reach out with it on Sunday mornings. It was also for the AWANA program. I also used it to take the youth to the all-night, Word of Life rallies and occasionally took the senior saints to Blair Factory Outlet in Pennsylvania. That was always a nice trip! Things seemed to be going well. The church provided a beautiful parsonage with a garage and lots of lawn. It had a large weeping willow tree that Jason loved to climb up into a small tree house. He also liked to go fishing in the pond. Jason was a student down at Houghton College in their high school program. Jason was doing well in school, and he especially enjoyed basketball. Carla was at the same time going to the college with a major in music.

One day, I remember going up on one of the side roads to do some visitation. I was familiar with the area at that time, because I drove a school bus on the roads each day. I had gone to this one certain house and knocked on the door. A large burly man answered, and asked me what I wanted. I told him I was from the church there in town. He bid me to come into his house. We talked about the weather and different things and then I asked him if he went to church. He replied that he did occasionally. I then asked him if he knew Jesus as his Lord and Savior. His reply was that he thought he knew Jesus as his Savior. I asked him, if he had ever been baptized to be a witness of his faith. I will never forget his reply. He replied that he did not see any need for that, and I needed to leave because he had some things to do. I then proceeded to tell him what the Bible teaches regarding baptism. I told him that if it was good enough for Jesus, then we need to do it as well for a testimony of his faith and I left on that note.

About a week later on a Sunday morning we had this tall woman and two children that visited our church services. She had made out a visitor card and I did a follow up visit to her home. I soon realized that it was the same house where I had visited the week before. The large burly man! She invited me in and began to apologize for her husband. He at that same time came in from the kitchen. He also apologized telling me that what I had told him made him stop and think. His wife went on to tell me that they had had a quarrel a few nights before I had come. She was a Christian and that very day they had been arguing over his salvation. She had made sure there was a tract in the bathroom and they already had a latch on the outside of the door that locked. When he went into the bathroom, she had locked the door from the outside and told him he was not to come out until he was sure of his salvation. He had asked Jesus in his heart that night. He had previously only had "head knowledge" of Jesus. Since I was there, I went over the Romans Road (plan of salvation) and they both wanted to reassure their faith and recite the sinner's prayer. He then looked at me and asked me when he could get baptized. It was two weeks later, on a Sunday night while we were at Hume Baptist church for a hymn sing, that I baptized both of them. The reason we did the baptism at Hume Baptist is that Hunt Baptist where I was pastor did not have a baptismal. The Hume Baptist church where we went that night not only had the hymn sing but a baptismal. There were different churches in the area that got together once a quarter to have a hymn sing, and this time they witnessed the baptism.

This latest episode made me realize that God is the Great Shepherd. I could be a pastor, which is a little shepherd. He is the one that, through the Spirit, draws all men, causes things to be as they are, and makes all things new! What a great feeling I had just being a part of this couples salvation, since I had been away from church planting and church work for the last three years. It was good to be back in it again! This couple went on to study God's Holy Word in their home on Tuesday evenings.

Patti and I had begun a new Bible Study up at the new church member's house with a few of their neighbors and some teens. They were eager to learn the Word of God. We had eight regular attendees. We also had a Bible Study with a young married couple in town and another with two deacons in their home. Bible studies, where people were growing in the Word of God, Sunday services that were growing with new members, a rather large AWANA program; and Saturday morning basketball with Jason and his friends in the church gym kept us busy. These programs were a major outreach in the community. There were many exciting things happening. It would seem that everybody should have been happy in the work of the Lord. However, we soon found out that Satan was alive and well!!

The deacons asked me to come to a special meeting at the church. The deacon board informed me that they did not appreciate some of the kids who were coming to Sunday school. They were rude, not neat in their appearance and ran in the church. I began to explain that as far as I was concerned, all children should be able to come to church and that Christ would want that. They went on to let me know that it was their church and that they built it!

It was very evident that my ministry there and the work that God had given to me, was a great blessing. It was very evident however that the greatest of all enemies the Devil himself was at work. One of the things I wanted to do was to have another vote of confidence. I won the vote with 80% of the total votes. However, it was made very clear to me in the following months that if I stayed the church would split. Personally, I did not want that to happen as it would leave a bad mark on the community. Therefore, I resigned my position as pastor of that church and what happened next would be a pleasant surprise! God is always preparing us for the next step of the journey. The road we travel in our Christian walk has already been prepared by the Lord. All we need to do is to learn the lessons that God is teaching us. We then need to go on to the next destination with Him knowing that He is leading. Moses in Exodus knew that God was moving him and the nation of Israel forward even when the way looked impossible! They could not go back! They could only go the way that He was leading them. Lord, where is our next destiny?

"Anywhere with Jesus I can safely go!"

19

RICH BLESSING, AND PEACE OF GOD!

Patti's sister, Kathy Ray, had told us a while back that their pastor had resigned and left the church. It was a relatively new work at the time. The church was a new building with 15 acres of land and plenty of room for growth. I was not in the least bit interested in being a pastor of another church! I did want to serve the Lord though. This particular church was small in numbers and somewhat like a Bible study group. I believe their were about 30 people. Patti, Jason & I were just happy worshipping with them.

In the previous chapter, I had mentioned that I drove a school bus. However, after one year of this, and many problems between students on the bus and their parents, I decided to quit that job. I had 30 plus years with a chauffeur's license and a spotless record. I had an offer for a job driving for the county. It was through the Hillside Industries program, (A.R.C.). I would be taking handicap individuals back and forth to work, plus doing the field trips. It was not long, before they had me doing many, many excursion trips with these people. I mention all this to you for the sake of the fact that I had an income. Patti was also working as a nurse doing home health work. Most of the time, she had "high tech" cases. We were making a living, but not actually in the Lord's work. God was about to make a big change in this! Patti & I were very much involved at the time with a local pastor's group. We pastors and wives would meet once a month to pray and share with each other regarding the ministries that God had called us all to work in for Him. It was at one of these meetings that one of the pastors approached me to consider taking the pastorate of the church where he was in Little Valley, New York. It would not be far from the Indian reservation my grandfather was from. One Sunday we took a drive down to their church, met some of the people, and spent time with the pastor and his wife. It was a pretty yet very rural country area for sure. They did have one factory there that made the paper spun lollipop sticks for different candy companies in many countries. I had never seen a factory like that before, and have not seen one since! It was a great weekend!

We were just resting and waiting on God while we enjoyed our worshipping at Pleasant Valley Baptist Church. After many years in the ministry, it seemed nice! I did get a chance to preach occasionally and I taught Sunday school occasionally. It was only two weeks, from the time we had visited the other church, that we received a letter asking us to come and candidate there. I had been thinking that the last 10 months were a nice vacation! Patti & I decided to go back down to Little Valley Baptist church and candidate as God seemed to have opened the door. It was a great weekend, especially because there was an Indian family that visited for the first time. The Salamanca Indian reservation was only a few miles from that church. Since I am part Indian myself, this really made the whole weekend exciting!

Meanwhile, when we got back to Pleasant Valley, they informed us that they seemed to be very interested in having us as well. We received word three days later, that the church down in the other valley also wanted me to be their pastor. We began to pray, about God's will as He had opened two doors of ministry. Pleasant Valley wanted us to candidate there. It was about the eleventh month that we had been with them. Our hearts were thrilled that God had opened a ministry to us again! Now we have two choices. We decided to candidate right there at Pleasant Valley where we lived, simply because we already knew the people. The weekend that I was to candidate, Gertie Peer, an old friend from Wellsboro, Pa. was visiting us. She had come to see the lovely little village of Lakeville where we lived. The village is located on the north end of Conesus Lake. As I previously mentioned, the pastor, and three of his children from her church in Wellsboro, Pa., were killed by a drunk driver. She was one of the families that knew what had happened there. She knew that I was going to candidate, and wanted to be there that particular Sunday as well. After I had preached, I advised the people there that I would only accept their vote if it turned out to be 100% in my favor. While I visited some of the people, I noticed that the deacons took Gertie in one of the Sunday school rooms. In fact, Patti, Jason and I waited for them to finish talking with her because she rode with us. We then all went home to eat lunch. Apparently, the deacons had wanted to ask her some questions as to all she knew about me.

The following weekend was when Pleasant valley Baptist Church was going to vote on whether to have me come and be their pastor. Patti, Jason and I went away that Sunday to Patti's younger sister's house. We went to church in our old home church, North Brookfield Baptist. After church when we were about half way through our meal, the telephone rang and my sister-in-law told me that it was for me. My brother in law Don Ray, who was one of the deacons, told me that the vote from the people of the church was in. I had gotten 101% of the vote! It was because one of the people who was unable to be at the church that Sunday, had stopped by the church and left her vote in an envelope to be read when the vote was counted. WOW! God sure had called my bluff! God had answered above and beyond, what my expectation was. I believe that it was the first time in my life that I had ever heard of a church having a 100% vote for a pastor. Thank you God! I was to start the first Sunday of the next month. I had only two weeks to prepare! This was exciting because I already knew the people. I had been observing them and they had been observing Patti and I.

The ministry was a good one! They could not afford to pay me full time, so I still drove bus part time as well. The driving usually consisted of 20-35 hours a week. Occasionally it would be 40 plus hours.

I was busy and able to drive bus, which I liked to do. I also was able to do ministry to people and preach which I liked to do as well. I began home Bible studies with some of the members, and occasionally there would be a visitor. Patti got involved in a Clothes Closet ministry in the church and her sister Kathy helped with organizing a Food Pantry. These were open to the public each week with great success. I had gotten involved in the community with the local chapter of Rotarians. One of the other pastors in the area helped start a jail ministry in the local jail. We were involved with both of these ministries. The deacons and I did some door to door visitation and one of them did our monthly, news letter for the church. His wife set-up and maintained our church library. We also had a ministry through the local radio station. The church began to grow in numbers, and baptisms were quite common. I thought that we were penetrating the community very nicely!

One day I received a call from one of the Mount Morris funeral homes. They had a family that had a death. The problem at the time of the call was, the local pastor had not handled the situation very well and the family was upset. They had called the undertaker to find a different pastor. He called me, simply because I had met him at the local Rotarian meeting. I told him that I would be glad to meet with the family. To make a long story short, I did just that. Precious people had given their lives to the Lord that day and the family was happy. The funeral was great! It ended up that I received calls from that funeral home many times! I greatly appreciated this. I would rather do a funeral any day than do a wedding. Man, you can really preach the gospel at a funeral! It causes many people to have an open mind as to where their eternal destination is.

It seemed that the ministry I had here was wide open for God to do a work in! It was all a pastor could hope for and then some. WOW, what a great ministry God had given me. I began to do a counseling ministry with different bus drivers at the shop where I worked. Some of the people on the bus had me counsel with them. In fact, some of them came and joined the church. The people were coming from the community, the bus route, and the funeral homes. It was exciting to see it all! Patti also had many people coming to the clothes closet and food pantry. The number was growing month by month.

There were also some interesting little things that let me know that God had a sense of humor. I had a young man by the name of Dan Slater in the church that led my music. His dad was our pastor back in the North Brookfield Baptist church, when Patti & I were teenagers. His dad had counseled us many times and helped us during our teen years. He was a great pastor. In fact, his Dad had married us, and his mom sang at our wedding ceremony. This was back in 1963, when we were married back in our old home church (North Brookfield Baptist). Dan was a very young boy! Now, God had brought him here to Pleasant Valley Baptist and he led all my music. His mom actually came occasionally to play piano for us when we needed a substitute piano player. Dan's wife, Gloria, sang duets with him, played guitar, and sang in our praise band.

There was one couple, and one woman that handled our group of teens. They all were involved with our ministry of pantomimes. They would play a musical c.d., and act out plus sign for the deaf, the words of the songs. They were quite good at it and went to different places to do their programs. One of the places they enjoyed going was the local nursing home. Since we had a very good music program and the pantomime ministry, the nursing home folks liked that.

One of the ministries in the church was the church library. This was a big aspect for many of the people who could not buy Christian books. It was a large library, which took up one whole wall in the sanctuary. Not only, were there many, many books, but there were taped messages, cassettes of music, children's programs and video's including the whole collection of the Bill Gaither music videos. It was a very nice library and neatly taken care of by one of our senior ladies. Her husband George Larson had been interim pastor before we came, and was a big help to me in the transition period.

So, as you can tell by now, there were many good things happening around the Pleasant Valley Baptist Church. Between the outreaches and the ministries within, things were going very well, thanks to the

Lord Jesus Christ! The church was built by Southern Baptist Church, and was part of the Rochester, New York Baptist Association. They held to an independent position. I did go to a couple monthly meetings. (Even though the church knew that I was Independent Baptist) Dan went as well because he was on the Board of Counsel. Once a month, the association would sponsor an old fashion hymn sing. All the churches of the association would meet in one of the churches for this. Many of the churches took part and provided special music such as solos, duets, trio's, quartets etc. It was always fun! Patti and I really loved God's work here! It was wonderful compared to the ministries that we had previously been in since leaving the Philippine Islands.

As I have already mentioned, the bus driving was a great way to meet and counsel different people including drivers and riders. The owner and operator of the Bus Company had me doing many different routes. I asked him one day about it and he replied that he had watched my time on each of the different runs. It seemed that I was able to do many of them in less time than some of the other driver's. He checked into the situation, and had discovered that some of the drivers were just abusing the time. Therefore, since I was trust- worthy of my time, and had at that time, 30 plus years driving with a spotless Chauffeurs License, he would eventually have me doing most of the special trips. This proved to be so!

My second year there I began driving many of their long road trips. I really loved doing those and was able to enjoy, and see many different places. I would go to the state parks for picnics, the Buffalo Bills training sessions, the Rochester Red Wing baseball games and also up to the Buffalo waterway for boat cruises where we would see and smell the Nabisco Cereal Factory. However, this really took much of my time. Between driving and the church ministries, I had not realized fully what had been happening.

Now, we all know that there are only so many hours in a week. My weeks at that time were consisting of roughly 65-70 hours per week. (I found this out later) In fact, I never realized this until my health began to crumble. I was taking much pain medication and I was tired much of my free time. I fell asleep in my chair a lot. Yet, I would not have even noticed it so much, if it were not for what God allowed to happen next!

God can get our attention in many ways! (I will explain it all in the next chapter!

20

STRUCK DOWN...BUT NOT FORSAKEN!

God's ways are not our ways! He is the one that "directs our path" (Proverbs 3:5-6.) He takes us on a path sometimes that leads down into the valley. It is in the valley that He restores our souls, and shows us His tender mercy and grace. This is what He did with me and it has changed my life completely!

My life took a dramatic change one-day as I was in the bus garage at the shop. I had gone up the 8 foot ladder to retrieve my clipboard that was in the bus. I needed the clipboard because I was to do a road trip with a different bus. It was a cold and wet January in New York, and I had rubber overshoes on. As I was backing out of the bus door onto the ladder, my rubber overshoe slipped off the first step of the ladder. This caused me to have a great fall, 8 feet to the cement floor below. I immediately stood up, picked up my hat and brushed off the dirt from my jacket. I had landed on my right shoulder, which also caused me to hit my head on the right side.

One of the mechanics and the shop secretary came to see if I was all right. I felt a bit stunned, and told them that I was all right. It appeared to me that I was alright. I proceeded with the other bus run. I did go to V. A. and get some pain medication later that day. I began taking a lot of pain medicine (Naproxen) at that time. For the next few days I seemed to be doing fair to well. I assumed that the stiffness and pain I was having at the time was only because of my aching bones. My supervisor told me that I needed to go see their doctor that they used for injuries at the shop. I responded with the fact that I was going to Buffalo Veterans Administration Hospital the next afternoon for a workup of my back and would need the afternoon off from work to do that. My thinking was that I had never used Worker's Compensation in my life and I did not want to start. However, my supervisor told me that it would be in my best interest to apply for it now.

I went to the Buffalo Veterans Administration Hospital where they checked me out. They told me that I was to continue on the Naproxen. They also told me that I would have to go through extensive therapy on my right arm and shoulder. I was to go to the Veterans Administration Hospital in Canandaigua, New York, where there was a therapeutic pool. The Arthritis foundation of Rochester, New York also used this pool. The V. A. Hospital felt that the warm water would be especially good for my spine and my shoulder. It was in August, that VA did a rotator cuff operation on my right shoulder. (I had one three years before this) The result was, I got infection in my shoulder really bad! It was full of infection! It lasted eight weeks before it cleared up. This type of infection never fully leaves the body. Later, I would find this out.

Patti and I took a vacation that following January. We always went the last week of January through the first week of February. We always went down to Jacksonville, Florida for one week for a Pastors conference. We had been to the conference before and knew we would enjoy the great teaching and preaching. We always learned many new techniques for the ministry. The second week we did some sightseeing and visited old friends. However, that particular year, because of my fall, I was very uncomfortable. I could not stand comfortably and I could not sit comfortably, I did not sleep well at all. Something was very wrong. Even at the seminars that I attended, I had to stand with my spine against the doorframe and push into the sharp corner in order to relieve the pain at all. We made it back home, and began to get things checked out.

By the first week of March, I was not doing well at all and was really hurting! I headed out to do my bus run that particular morning as I always had done. On my first stop, I reached for the door handle to pull the bus door open, and realized I could hardly raise my arm up high enough to reach the handle. I also did not have strength enough to pull the door handle open after I lifted my arm with my left arm. I had to unbuckle my seat belt and use my left hand in order to open and shut the door. I managed to do the whole bus trip this way. Looking back, I wonder how I ever loaded two wheel chairs, which I always had on that run. After completing the bus run, I immediately went to Buffalo Veterans Administration Hospital and got checked out. They had me begin my pool therapy again. They realized that it was not doing as well as they had expected.

The compensation insurance finally went into effect, which we had applied for some time before this. From the time that I fell in January until the time I had applied, was supposed to be a ninety-day period. I had applied six days before the cutoff. Whew! Compensation insurance had me go to Strong Memorial Hospital in Rochester, NY for extensive shoulder therapy. However, this also did not bring about good results. They had a strength machine that measured the strength of your pull. My pull could not get up to the strength required to operate the opening and closing of a bus door which I needed to do to keep that job.

I was realizing that this was not good! I was on compensation, yet nothing had been done as of yet, regarding my spine. I began to inquire regarding this and soon was told, that I needed to see the bone and nerve specialist at Strong Memorial Hospital. Two weeks later I had an M.R.I. and many x-rays done. The doctor informed me that C-2, C-3, and C-4 of my spine were broken and almost severed. He then told me that just a bump or a jolt could either kill me or paralyze me from the neck down. It could kill me instantly. I told him about our trip to Florida and he really went berserk! He informed me that if any car had hit us in any way I would not be standing there before him. I shared with him that I have an awesome God who looks out for His children.

His response was that he also was a Christian, and that he wanted me to go to surgery as soon as his associate could schedule me.

The doctor did tell me that it would be a very serious operation. He informed me that most of the time it left the patient paralyzed from the neck down. Patti and I prayed and asked, "What now Lord," we need you to intervene? This meant that I would not be preaching for quite awhile. I had managed to keep preaching up to this point. We received word the next week that my surgery was set for that Monday morning after Easter. It was the day after Easter in 1999. It would be just over a year from my original fall.

Patti and I had taken out an insurance policy on us for catastrophic situations. I called the agent and he him came to our house the next night. He realized my situation of having no regular health insurance and that I only had the Veterans health plan to fall back on. He then told Patti and me that Blue Cross and Blue Shield could help us. We told him that we could not afford it. He then explained to us that they had a policy that if you had health insurance of any kind, they would have to grant me a full health policy since I did have catastrophe insurance which was insurance! He showed me their handbook and told us they would have to pick me up. He also advised me that I indeed had to make a compensation claim. The following day we went to the office of Blue Cross and Blue Shield. Now folks, you know that we went there only to get insurance, not give them our life history! They did not want to insure us. We then showed them their own handbook. After going back and forth with them, they finally told us that they would indeed insure us. This was great! We knew that there would be a premium, which we probably would not be able to pay. We praise the Lord because Pleasant Valley Baptist Church decided to pick up the premium for us since I was their pastor.

Meanwhile, the church had been growing and we were preparing for a large turnout for the Easter Sunday morning. We had grown in numbers from over thirty, around ninety in just a few years. All five of our children had received word of my serious upcoming surgery and they were all going to be there that Easter Sunday. Let me tell you folks, I remember preaching as if I would never preach again that Easter Sunday! The church was packed. There were places to sit ninety people. I remember that there were people standing in the back of the church, and people standing in the hallway. They told me later that there were over one hundred in attendance that Sunday. It was a highlight and a great success! They all had told me on the way out of church that they would be praying for me, or that they would be at the hospital with Patti and my family, praying with them there.

The next morning my family and I headed to the hospital at 5:45 a.m. We were to be there by 6:00 a.m. The family went to the surgery waiting room while Patti and I proceeded into the pre-surgical rooms. I was not prepared for all of what they were going to do. Much of it was familiar to me. I did not know that they had to shave my head, and then they glued these strobes in different places on my scalp. That glue smelt worse than airplane hobby glue! They had me kiss my wife, and the doctor told them he was ready for me. I remember that they kept me awake until I was already on the surgical table. I then realized that my doctor wanted to pray with me before he operated. That was nice! Thus began my "first spinal surgery."

My surgery of the spine went very well, they told me. They had put in a bone graft from the bone bank. The next thing I remember was I had this terrible big tube down my throat. I could not talk or hardly respond to anything. There was a nice surprise waiting for me! They finally took me to my room in ICU. There were a couple of get well balloons hanging from the ceiling. A few minutes later, the nurse apparently realized from the monitor that I was stirring. She came in fixed the blanket and informed me that I must have been a very special person. She told me that there were over thirty people from our church downstairs in the lobby, and that they had brought large coolers with sandwiches; finger foods; and vegetables and soda plus water. They apparently had a big party! I later was told that they shared much of the food with other people there, and even shared the gospel. WOW! Even in my surgery, the testimony of our church was spreading.

Meanwhile, I had this large "halo" screwed into my head. They really should have called it a crown of thorns. The attached vest came all the way down my torso. Tubes and hoses were everywhere. After three days a team of doctors came into my room and proceeded to take the tracheotomy out. That helped me be a bit more comfortable! Then, on the forth day, they took me out of Intensive Care Unit and put me in a private room since nothing else was available. This was nice! Realizing I was out of the "worst" of it, Patsy's family had to go back to Michigan which made me a bit sad. I seemed to be doing better than they thought I would. Instead of the normal stay of two weeks that it usually took, they sent me home that Friday afternoon. Since my wife is a nurse, she could do the I.V. She also could help me get up to the bathroom plus help me with my food. She was, and still is a "trooper of a nurse!"

The following Wednesday I began to have what I thought was a severe sinus headache. Nothing seemed to relieve it. When my wife came home from her home health assignment, she gave me some Vicks to put in my nose to help. By the evening, there was not much relief. I remember praying and asking God why I could not get rid of this headache. Patti went upstairs to bed. I was trying to sleep in the lift chair that I had been using. My brother-in-law Don Ray had borrowed it from his uncle. However, I did not sleep much because of the severe headache. I know that I saw the time right up till 3:00 a.m. Then I must have fallen to sleep. That was the last I remember. Apparently, Patti got up the next morning and tried to wake me for the bathroom and to see what I wanted to eat for my breakfast. I later found out that she tried to slap me and still could not wake me. She called the ambulance and they loaded me in to take me to the hospital. I managed to hear a question from one of the workers as to who was the president. Like, who cares in that state of mind! I do not remember anything else until I had already undergone emergency surgery.

I found out that the bone graft they put in was infected and the infection had spread into the spine, causing a major problem. They had rushed me back to the hospital where I proceeded to have a spinal tap. I had to lay, in the emergency room, on the cot from that morning until almost midnight. I certainly did not know or remember it. The hospital could not get in contact with my doctor, and he was the only one they had, who specialized in this spinal cord surgery. The doctor did finally arrive and the bone graft that he had put in last week was now going being removed. My body had some of that infection from my shoulder lying dormant in there. The doctor had to clean, and disinfect the whole area in my neck and spine. I now had to be in traction for ten days with heavy antibiotics. Thus was my "second spinal cord surgery."

I then laid in traction for ten days. I could not sit up for any reason. I had to manage to eat, sleep, and do everything, while lying flat on my back. I remember that they had young nurses in training and candy striper nurses who came in to bathe and feed me. It was good training for many of them since they would probably never have anything quite like this "halo" again in their careers. It was also quite embarrassing to me. Something else I remember quite well about those ten days was that one afternoon my doctor's assistant came in with an assortment of things. He gave me three injections in the scull. Man that really hurt! That was only the half of it! He then proceeded to put more screws in the band of my halo and turned them into my scalp. Patti said she could almost see the sheet under me as I was almost off the bed from the pain. I tell you that really hurt!

After the ten days of traction, the doctor came and told me that he had to go back in and clean out the infection again and put me back in traction. Thus was my "third spinal cord surgery!" That went well, and he came back two days later and showed me a piece of titanium that he was working with. After going on the inter net, and talking with a European doctor, he had come across this interesting three inch piece of titanium that he had made. He then took me for my "fourth spinal cord surgery." He cleaned out the rest of the infection and put in the temporary piece of titanium that would act like my spine.

I then was on a large amount of antibiotics. He kept me there in the hospital for one week and the following Monday, I went home with an I.V. with Patti and some special instructions. One thing we had to get was an R.N. to come in and check the I.V. in case there developed infection around it. Plus, she put the shipment of IV's in the refrigerator each week and made sure Patti was doing o.k. Thus, three weeks of this routine went by. It was a relief to Patti to have the nurse as well, since she shouldered a lot of responsibility at that time. I would be at home on the I.V. antibiotics for two weeks. Two weeks in the hospital, and two at home, made a total of four weeks. On Friday of the second week at home, my doctor called and advised me to be at the hospital the next Monday morning at 6:00 am.

We arrived on time and preceded to what I now knew to be familiar territory. As I was being prepared for what was now to be my "fifth spinal cord surgery." The doctor advised me that he would be taking out the temporary piece. He then would take a piece of bone from the side of my leg called the tibias bone. He would take a piece about the length and size of my little finger and shape it to the titanium graft that he took out, which meant I would be using my own bone. I can honestly say that this was a great success! The operation went very smoothly and my recovery went well. My only draw back was, not only the spine needed to recover from the surgery, but now I have a leg hurting, and it had to recover from surgery as well. I had to learn to bear weight on the leg again. I was learning to walk, learning how to speak (because of surgery through the throat), and learning how to function with my arm and hand. I had lost the use of my right arm and hand because of nerve damage. I know that the Lord was with me, because I know that from the neck down, could easily have been paralyzed. I was happy that this was all I had wrong with me. I spent a total of three weeks in therapy before I was able to come home. As you can picture it, I was in the hospital more than I was home for a few months now!

I am happy to say that many of the church people were with me throughout all the ordeals. They stood with Patti and me through "thick and thin"! They are great people whom I loved very much and still do. It was now time for me to get back to a little work. Never in my life had I been so long out of work. The doctor gave me permission to preach on Sundays.

I was in the office two weeks after my discharge from the hospital and I felt good. As I was preparing for the next Sunday's message, the telephone rang. When I turned and reached for the telephone to answer it, something in my neck snapped. I could hardly move. I had just seen my doctor in his office two days before this. I knew he that he was there, so I called him. He advised me to go to the hospital emergency room where he would meet me. I called Patti at her work and she came picked me up at the church and off we went! After an M.R.I. and some x-rays, the doctor told me that he was going to have to operate again. The bone graft had shifted just enough to push on a nerve, and this was the cause of the problem that I was experiencing. "Thus, my sixth spinal cord surgery" was administered. What he did on that operation, he put me in a sling on my belly. He was to go into the back of my throat to the spinal cord. Since he had me on my belly, he was able to operate on the back of my spine easier. He attached a small plate with two screws to hold the bone graft from slipping again. This was not so severe an operation, and I was home in only four days. Now, dear reader, you would think that God had put me through enough would you not? *"He will not take us through anything, but what His grace sustains us."*

Things went along well from the end of July, August, September, and into October. Then my great day of freedom finally had come for the doctor to take off the halo. What a relief! However, I had to learn to walk again. I no longer had that big heavy halo to balance. I was really tipsy for a while. I was finally back and able to do more than I had for tosix months. I will never know why they called it a halo. It was more like a crown of thorns! Another disappointment was the selling of our motorcycle. Patti and I enjoyed that bike a lot. Now that I am an incomplete quadriplegic, I could not balance the bike well. I really did not want to sell it.

I realized how fortunate I was to have a church that stood behind me. I also thanked God everyday that I was not a complete paralyzed individual. Sure, I had lost feeling in my right side, and the thumb and two fingers of my left hand were numb a lot. However, Lord, I want to thank you for getting me through what was a great deep valley.

December came, that year, and Patti, Jason and I were excited that "dear old Dad" was going to be around for it! The second week of December I began to experience a lot of pain again in my spine. I did not know whether I had nerves that were trying to come back to life or what. The doctor checked me out at the Hospital with another M.R.I. and more x-rays. He concluded that the bone graft had slipped. It was because of deterioration in my spine. The sections were in bad shape. His only hope for me now was to have two six inch rods placed down each side of the spine with twelve screws, which together would hold the bone graft from moving anymore. "Thus my seventh spinal cord surgery"! This surgery went very well. I did not even have pain medication! The nurse kept asking if I wanted some, and I continued to let them know I did not need any. I went home the following Monday with a bone density contraption hooked up to my spine. This was two weeks before Christmas. It all started with a reconstruction of a shoulder that was "blown apart" in the fall I took. Then, there were seven spinal surgeries. That totaled eight surgeries in thirteen months!

I can honestly say, dear reader, that seven is God's number of perfection! But Lord, did you need to take me through all seven? I realized that *"God is too wise to make a mistake! His ways are to perfect!"* The following March I developed severe heart problems again. I underwent a series of tests only to find out that the lower right quadrant of my heart, where it consists of all small capillaries, had shut down completely. They called it post...traumatic stress of the heart from all the surgeries. The only thing that they could do was medicine control. They also put me into a heart study program. After four weeks of the "perfect" study, they decided that I was failing their study. Medicine was the only option I had. They told me that it was because of the stress from all the spinal surgeries. Finally on my records they called it "post -traumatic stress symptom" of the heart. I am glad that they could at least get me onto some real good heart medicine.

My friends, God has brought me through the deepest valley that I can comprehend. I trust and I pray that none of you readers have to ever go through such a valley. If you do…remember that God can do the same for you! I know that my God has not only brought me down into the valley, He never, never, left me, ---not even in the valley. He has brought me out, and then, back up on the hillside. Praise his Name! All I can do is to say, "Rejoice in the Lord always; and again I say, rejoice! (Philippines 4:4)

Patti and I have been to the Philippine Islands three times. We have driven across the United States four times. We have seen many things. We have experienced the good times and the bad times. Nothing had compared to what I went through that two years of time. Yet, we have found God to be the only sure foundation in this. *"God can make a way when there seems to be no way!"*

I trust dear reader that you have taken Jesus as your personal Lord and Saviour. I trust that He as **Lord** of your life. The Bible clearly tells us that all have sinned and come short of His glory (Romans 3:23). "The wages of our sin is death [hell] but the gift of God is eternal life through Jesus Christ our Lord." (Romans 6:23) The Bible tells us, "that if thou shalt confess with thy mouth the Lord Jesus, and shalt believe in thine heart that God has raised Him from the dead, thou shalt be saved. For with the heart man believeth unto righteousness; and with the mouth confession is made unto salvation." (Romans 10:9-10) "Whosoever shall call upon the name of the Lord shall be saved." (Romans 10:13) "For God so loved the world (You) that He gave His only begotton Son, that whosoever believeth in Him should not perish, but have everlasting life." (John 3:16) Jesus told us, "No man shall be able to pluck them out of my hand…" (John 10:28-30)

Our journey of life has not been boring! It is all because of Christ that we made it this far!

21

IT'S ALL BECAUSE OF CALVARY!

Shortly after I had failed the heart study, I had an appointment with my family physician. She wanted to review the results of the heart study. It was on a Tuesday. After a short time she came out from her office. I will never forget what she told me. She informed me that my heart condition was not good and it only had 46% of it is function. I thanked her that I was glad to hear I had 46% of my heart. She was not impressed! Then she began to explain all the details of the findings, not only of the heart, but also of the spinal paralysis. She advised me that if the Sunday coming up was not my last Sunday to preach, it could very well be my last Sunday. "Mr. Pierce, you need to step down from the ministry, buy a camper and enjoy and yourself the remaining few years that you have." I must tell you that this was quite a shock! That meant that in five days…I would have to quit what I loved to do. (If I had to do it over, I would have had a meeting with the deacons.)

That next Sunday, I preached and proceeded to read a letter that I had prepared. I then had officially resigned my position at the church. They were just as shocked, as I had been when the doctor told me what she wanted me to do. There were many tears that Sunday morning. I, of course, had a very hard time with it all.

It was about one week later that I took Patti over to Avon for lunch at a little diner there we liked. When we finished eating and we were standing at the front counter to pay for our lunch, I noticed that across the highway was a small car dealership. What caught our eye was a nice 27' used motor home. We went over and looked through the windows and Patti immediately liked the light blue interior. In fact, it even had plastic on the swivel chair that was part of the living room area. I noticed that it had brand new tires, and it was very nice! A man came out and told us that he was the owner of the shop. He informed us that he had just gotten it at the car auction the night before. He then gave me all the particulars about it so that I could go to my bank and make a deal if I was interested.

I went to the bank the next day and discovered that it was worth much more than he had paid at the auction. Therefore, I got the money from the bank then went back to Avon, and paid what the dealer wanted for it. The Lord had allowed us to get the motor home for $3000 less than it was valued. It was a 1987 Coachman Crusader with only 27,000 miles on it. It only had one previous owner. I got his name from the original title and found out that he was 87 years old, that his wife had died and they only had used it to go back and forth to Florida from New York. God gave us a great deal!

Dear reader, do you remember me telling you way back in one of the early chapters of this book that I was saved at age 13, at an old fashion tent revival? It was in the town of Chaffee, New York, next to Odasagah Bible Conference grounds. The word "Odasagah," is an Indian name meaning "Living Water." It is not far from the Indian reservation of my ancestors. At this conference grounds they have a place to park your campers for weeks, months, or a year at a time. Patti and I went up there for most of the summer that year. I really loved the relaxing atmosphere. I got lots of rest and time for reading, listening to good fundamental preaching from the Word of God, in the morning. There was good old fashion gospel preaching each night with special music. Many times, they would have Southern Gospel music quartets. They have a small lake there for fishing, water sports, boat cruises, and water-skiing. If you liked, and you were able, you could pitch horseshoes and play tennis or miniature golf. There were many things there to keep a family busy. If you did get tired of cooking, you could go to their cafeteria for breakfast, lunch, or supper. After the evening service, they often had the ice cream shop open. We really loved that summer! I was able to rest a lot and get my strength back.

In July of that year, Pleasant Valley Baptist hosted a retirement party for me. It was outside in the pavilion that we had built a few years earlier. When I arrived that day, I could not believe the number of people there! They came from all over. People from churches that had supported us while when we were on the field as their missionaries. Many of the community organizations had representatives there as well. It was a fabulous job that the church did that day. There were skits and special music, then came a big surprise to me. They awarded me with a large plaque for 28 years of faithful ministry! WOW! They also gave me an envelope that, when I arrived home, I found that it contained enough money for me to buy a new computer. Praise God! (I never had a computer, only a word processor.) Not only did Patti and I get the joy of serving Him, but, God always pays back way more than we deserve!

Winter, for me, that year was extremely difficult. We lived, (as I have already mentioned), on the north end of Conesus Lake. We had to back the motor home up by the living room windows to block the wind. This helped to keep our living room just a bit warmer. From the third week of December, through the second week of February, it was 0 degrees to -20 degrees below zero every day and every night. Each time someone opened up our living room door to go in or out, the plate, screws, and rods in my neck would tighten up and ache like a bad tooth- ache. I did not go out of the house for about two months. On the week of Christmas our oldest daughter Patsy, her husband and their three teenage boys came home to celebrate the Christmas Holiday with us. I thought that surely they would be all right in the motor home with the gas furnace. Well, they froze the first night, so we put an electric heater in there as well. They still had an awful time keeping warm. It was just plain freezing!

Our furnace in the house ran constantly! The fuel bill was

outrageous! It was a rough winter, to say the least. Even on the second week of March, we had a blizzard that dumped over 5 feet of snow, burying the car. It took Patti and a neighbor a whole day to dig it out, only to realize we could not go anywhere!

I sure was glad when the warm weather finally came. In May, I got the motor home serviced and ready to roll. By May 10th, I went back out to Odasagah Bible Conference Center. Patti came out on the weekends, as she worked during the week. It sure helped my disability check, and since Patti had to update her car. I was able to get her a '95 Olds Cutlass Cierra. I got a great deal on it and it was spotless!

It was in my third week there at Odasaga that I had exhausted my reading material and took a nap one afternoon. When I woke up, I realized that I was ready to do something besides this. The evening meeting was another 4 hours away. I could not read any more because I had read all I had. I picked up the Liberty Baptist Journal and realized I had read all the articles, and so I decided to read the advertisements in the back. At least I had not read them. I really did not need to buy anything. Well, as I was reading down the second column, I noticed this 1 inch by 1 inch advertisement that read like this: "Wanted, retired pastor to work one day a week with seniors." God caused a light bulb to go off in my head! I always knew that there was never a full retirement package specified for pastors in the Bible. Sure, I loved this place, but if there happened to be anything that I could be doing for God, I sure would like to do it. Patti came that weekend and we prayed about it.

Sunday afternoon I packed up the motor home and headed home. Then, on Monday morning, I called my pastor, Pastor Ed Whitehead at our home church, North Brookfield Baptist Church. I left a message for him and that evening he called me back. I talked with him regarding the article, and he agreed that I probably could do it. He also was going to call the Pastor of the church (Buford Road Baptist) and talk with him letting him know of my health conditions.

I called the church in Richmond, Virginia the next day. The secretary would have the pastor, Dr. Tony Kohout, contact me that evening. He did call and talked with me a bit and wanted to know when Patti and I could come down to Richmond, VA. After talking with Patti it was decided that we would go down the third week of June. I was getting a bit excited! I felt better and wanted to serve God any way He would allow me.

We did go down to Richmond, and we met with Pastor Tony Kohout of the Buford Road Baptist Church. Things went very well! He was able to understand my situation as our pastor had already called him. Pastor John DePugh of Newark Baptist Fellowship Church, (where I spoke for revival meetings), had also sent him a letter. Buford Road Baptist Church put us up in the Comfort Inn for both Saturday and Sunday nights. Pastor Kohout and his wife Gail took us out for lunch and dinner, so our expenses down there were covered. We enjoyed the Sunday services, and met many of the people, especially many of the senior saints. Then Pastor Tony asked Patti and I when we could move down. We let him know that we needed to go back home and pray about it. Well, God was moving and we knew it quite well.

The 5th of July I came down and met with one of the seniors, Mr. Cecil Rock. Another man by the name of Lonnie Raines met us as well. They took me around the area sightseeing. The main objective was to look at housing. After a bit, they told me they had to go to the office. Well, their office was at the Hardy's, for breakfast! We then proceeded to a mobile home park that they knew of. They took me to a three-bedroom mobile home that someone from the church was selling. It seemed cramped for me because of the way it was designed.. We then drove around to the other end of the Park. Lonnie advised me that I probably would not be interested in the mobile home they were about to show me, but I probably should at least look at it. When we came around the corner and I saw it, I knew that it was nice looking. It had a nice deck and yard. When we went inside, the living room was large! The dining area had a big armoire. The two bedrooms were on opposite ends, and each one had a full bath. It also had central air. This was nice! I talked with the owner, who happened to be there, and found out the price of the mobile home. I made a deal on it right then! I had to go back to the motel and call my Annuity Board to get the down payment for her. The rest we would try to pay by the first week of August. We now had housing in Richmond, VA. I then headed back home to New York. I bought it without Patti with me!

Patti and I started packing and many of the church people came by and helped. Our target date was set to move the last week of August. We had three and a half weeks. There was much to do. The following week, from when I had secured the mobile home, the annuity board let me know that the rest of the money that I needed was available. However, the stock market had crashed and I was $1000 short of the amount I needed. I was to leave the following Monday morning to go back down to Richmond and finish paying the owner. She had to be out of the mobile home and needed the money to finish paying what she owed.

That Monday I arrived at the church in Richmond. Cecil Rock was waiting for me. When I got in his truck, he asked me if I had all of the money I needed. I told him that I was short the amount. He gave me an envelope that contained $300 that the senior's Sunday school class had put together. This still left $700 to come up with. He was a bit disturbed about the fact that I was still short the money needed. I told him that many times in the Bible, God's people had to step out by faith if they were sure God was in what they were doing. We went to see the owner of the mobile home and talked with her. Her husband advised her that it would be all right if I was willing to pay $100 a month for the seven months for the remainder. So we signed the deal and I gave her the annuity check that I had already signed. She had us go to her bank, but they were not willing to accept the out of town check. Cecil was really talking now! It was 4:30 on Monday afternoon. He then took me to the Bank of America where one of the church members worked as a supervisor. The annuity check was a check from the Bank of America in Texas. The woman that he was looking for was not there, but one of the other supervisor's, was there. He took care of the matter for us. They gave me a cashier's check, which I took back to the owner of the Mobile Home.

It was great to see how God worked it all out! Cecil Rock thought that the whole day was an exciting one. We went back to the church where we prayed and thanked God for moving the mountains, and then I headed back home to New York!!

Cecil Rock, Lonnie Raines, and George Burnham from the church all arrived the last week of August with a Budget Rental Truck. The Buford Road Baptist Church sent them with the truck to move us. They covered the cost, which was nice! Jason, Patti and I left the following day, since some of the church people from Pleasant Valley Baptist wanted to meet us for breakfast the next morning. We left for Richmond about 9:30 a.m. with the motor home full of boxes and the Toyota pick-up half full on a car dolly.

Jason was a big help in getting us settled into our new home. He had come home to help us move. It was sad when we took him to the airport. He needed to get back to his Marine base located in San Diego, California. Patti and I headed back to our home and to our new ministry. It was not going to be too large a job as I was only supposed to work one day a week. The ministry was to start that next Tuesday morning. However, the second Tuesday when we met I will never forget! It was the morning of 9/11. We spent much of our time in prayer for the President and our great country. What a way to start this ministry!

I was able to do a good job teaching, heading up our trips, sightseeing, going to Quartet Concerts, teaching in the Bible Institute, plus visitation and hospital calls that needed to be made. This was a lot more than one day a week. It soon took its toll on my health and I was back in the hospital twice. The third year was even worse for me. The medicine for pain called Oxycodone was causing me to get things confused and I was not myself. I went into the hospital again with a heart attack and a severe stomach ulcer that the doctors did find out that all the pain medication that I had been taking was probably the cause.

After three years, it was evident that I had to resign my position at the church as senior director. We still go to their meetings and have special friends there. Even one couple from the church, Jim and Dana Hess, came over and eat with us on Friday or Saturday evening and play Skip-Bo.

I have since preached revival meetings in Newark Valley, New York and have led the senior devotions when they allow me. I love serving Jesus and will serve Him until the day I die. I hope to do pulpit supply, teach, preach, or even do mission conferences if I have a chance. Any door that God opens, I know that God knows my condition and will give me the health and strength to do it. As of this writing, I am doing volunteer work in the chaplain service at the local Veterans Administration Hospital. I am also a Peer counselor in their spinal cord ward, encouraging and helping the men to overcome their handicaps. I am ready to help anyone, anytime with Gods grace. I have been elected Chaplain of the American Legion. It is a clean group of men and women and there are a few Christians in the group. I keep doing what I can for my Lord and master. I want to be busy for Him till I die.

God has led this country farm boy from the Unadilla Valley, and has led me around the world serving Him. I can only say, like the Happy Goodman's Gospel Quartet, "I Wouldn't Take Nothing for My Journey Now." And, "I Don't Regret a Mile I've Traveled for The Lord." These all apply to Patti & my ministry for the Lord as well. We left Bible College with one verse of Scripture on our hearts and it still is one of our dearest. It is found in the book of Joshua.

Joshua 1:8-9 "This Book of the Law shall not depart from your mouth, but you shall meditate in it day and night, that you may observe to do according to all that is written in it. For then, you will make your way prosperous and then you will have good success. Have not I commanded you, be strong and be of good courage; do not be afraid, nor be dismayed, for the LORD your God is with you wherever you go."

22

GODS TRULY AMAZING GRACE

One thing for sure is that when God calls you into ministry, that call is until you die or He calls you home. Therefore, I need to keep going in ministry of some kind until I die or Jesus comes.

I was counseling at the Veterans Hospital in Richmond and doing Bible Studies in our home for two years thinking that I was at least busy for Jesus. *God had other plans.*

I went into the Veterans hospital throwing up blood. I was so sick! After two days of vomiting and diarrhea I just asked God to take me home. That night I had the strangest dream and I can still remember it. It appeared that I was in heaven looking for Patti. There was this place people were going into like a big restaurant. They would not let me in. I told them I wanted to go in with my wife because I had a reservation. The person went in and after a short time came back out and told me Patti was not there yet. He also told me that we had reservations. Then he took me over by a tree and told me to look out over the vast valley. I saw many lights. I woke up and prayed that I might be a witness and lead more people to Jesus. "(He is the Light.)"

It was on a Wednesday that they released me from the hospital. At prayer meeting that night there was a missionary that spoke. He had this three door unit and told about going to Fairs and Festivals telling people about Jesus and many people get saved.

At the close of prayer I turned my power wheel chair and followed the pastor out to the vestibule as I often did. He shook my hand and told me that I could do that ministry in my wheel chair. He also mentioned that he would send a recommendation to the mission for me. Then, Mr. Jim Steed the missionary came to me and told me I could do the ministry of going to the fairs. In fact he had me come out to the Virginia State Fair where I began to be involved telling people of God's love. Jim had to leave because of health problems. I did not get discouraged because five young people came by and I was able to lead them to a saving knowledge of God's love. That was September 2007.

I realized that what I had dreamed in the hospital and what these men told me, that God was up to something in my life. I continued in my ministries and prayed, asking God about what He had shown me. It was not long that I became restless and told Patti I was going to fill out the application that Amazing Grace Mission had sent me. February of 2008 I received a phone call from Dr. Gardener and he told me everything in the application looked good and also told me to get involved in the fair ministry. It took Patti almost a year before she sent her application in. She also was accepted into the mission! We went to conference that year and were officially accepted into the mission at Landmark Baptist Church in Florida. What a wonderful church! If we were to have a home church in Florida it would be Landmark Baptist. The pastor preaches the Word without compromise. The people are so friendly! It is a wonderful church. Since 2008 while we are in Florida each year, we worship at Landmark Baptist.

In 2008 we did three fairs. Then, in 2009 we did 10 fairs and it gets better each and every step. There is no greater joy than showing people the way God wants them to go. In 2011 we did a total of 18 Fairs! That was a bit too much. We try to do about 15 – 16 fairs each year.

Some of the experiences that we have had are quite interesting. This one night we were just about to close up and this couple came to the booth. They were tattooed, and body pierced about every place you could imagine. He looked like he fell in a bucket of fish hooks. We showed them the 3-door unit and asked them if they were sure they'd go to heaven when they died. They wanted to know for sure so I asked them to step back to the table where I could show them from the Bible. They were hesitant about coming back but finally did. Then he looked at me and said, "So, now you are going to judge me." I said, "I cannot judge you!" The only one that can do that is Jesus. I was able to share the gospel with them and they received Jesus Christ as Savior. He jumped up and hugged me, and thanked me .Then he asked me, "What he should do with all this? (The tattoos and piercings)

I told him that it was between him and Jesus! All because we did not judge them! When we use the Scripture to show people what God says, we need to think about how we came to know Jesus. We come to Jesus just as we are. Some with fish hooks, some like me fat and not so nice looking. How did you come? Maybe you have not come to Jesus yet. He does not lie---He loves you; He does not change---He will always be there, always the same caring, loving way; He cannot let you come to the Father but by Him. You must ask Christ to save you from your sins in order to go to heaven. When you make it personal then it truly does become amazing grace!

Not only is there joy in sharing Jesus but, there is also some times that it is unpleasant. There are many people that do not want anything to do with the Gospel. They come by the booth and shout all kinds of things. I know that they did the same thing to Jesus. We have to realize that they are doing these things against Him not us. There have been times that they stop by and want to argue their thoughts. The first thing that I do is stop them and then tell them that what we believe (the Bible) is truth. What is there to argue! You either believe it or not. It still does not change the fact that it is truth.

God said it I believe it and that settles it. Joshua 1:8,

This Book of the law shall not depart out of thy mouth, but thou shalt meditate therein day and night, that thou mayest observe to do according to all that is written therein; for then thou shalt make thy way prosperous, and then thou shalt have good success. I Timothy 4: This is the walk of a good minister or (spokes-person) of Jesus Christ. Have your conduct "sanctified" by the Word of God and prayer. Verse

6, "nourished up in the Words of faith." Then, 4:15-16, Meditate upon these things; give thy self wholly to them; that thy profiting may appear to all. Taking heed unto thyself, and unto the doctrine; continue in them; for in so doing this thou shalt both save thyself, and them that hear thee.

God said it therefore I believe it and that settles it. Jesus taught us to take it to heart, therefore I'm going to! It is a faithful saying and worthy of all acceptation. John 1:1, "In the beginning was the Word, the Word was with God, and the Word was God."

We are not out there presenting ourselves. We represent the King of King and Lord of Lords!

It brings me to recall the time of Palm Sunday. When we begin to understand what Palm Sunday is all about. Tom Barnard writes, "The crowd that day was clueless. They never got it right. They shouted praises. He wept. They looked for a warrior-king riding a white stallion. They got a carpenter riding a donkey. They wanted hype. They got a healer. They wanted a prophet. They got one who fulfilled prophecy. They wanted a scepter. They got a Savior. They got nothing they asked for but everything they needed." Only they never really got it. They were clueless. Jesus was the only one there who really knew what was happening on that first Palm Sunday.

Just like those people that day in Jerusalem, we think we know what's going on, but we really don't have a clue. Jesus comes to our town and wants to help us; we don't even recognize Him for who He is. He wants our hearts. That is what it is all about.

Jesus! I can personally tell you that His Grace is truly amazing! I must ask you dear reader, are you 100% sure that you are going to Heaven when you die? John 3:16 tells us: "for God so loved the world (that's you and I) that He gave His only begotton Son (Jesus), that whosoever believeth in Him should not perish, but have everlasting life."

23

THANK YOU LORD!

One thing has become very clear to me. All that God has brought us through in our life has trained us for what we are doing today. The different churches we visit, and the different questions that many people have at the fairs are what we have experienced in our past ministry. Someone quoted, "God never moves without purpose or plan."

Patti & I always dreamed of traveling with an RV and enjoying our lives in our senior years. Never did we realize that God had it all planned out for us to do just that. Our present ministry of soul winning with Amazing Grace Missions allows us to travel where ever we wish to go. Although most of us have a regular route that we travel. We have fairs that we like to do each year. This is due partly because the churches know us and support the ministry. This all means God has blessed us with the ability to share Christ and His love, all the while traveling and sightseeing. America is really blessed with its beautiful mountains; lakes; and tourist attractions. West Virginia is our favorite state to see! I guess it is because of the many creeks and hollows like we had had back on the farm up the hollow. When I am driving, I like to see the beautiful mountains. Just to see all of what God made for us to enjoy.

I will let you know that the devil does not like us witnessing for Christ! It has appeared to us that the people we have coming through the fairs are much harder to reach for Christ than just a few years ago.

Even the children that come through will not accept a little smile tract. Then sometimes mothers will snatch the smile tract out of their child's hand and throw it back stating that they do not want their child exposed to religion. WOW! I would not let mine either if it was "religious." Jesus is a relationship.

What we try to do is to let them know that we are not religious. It is all based on a *relationship* with Christ. Jesus came and showed us God's love; died; rose again; was seen by many witnesses; ascended up to the Father in Heaven where He sits at the Fathers right hand making intersession for the Christian when we pray. It is all based on that relationship to Him. The only way that we have to Christ is when we ask forgiveness of our sins and accept Jesus as our personal Savior.

One of the most interesting places that we visit is Logan, WV. It is a quaint little town nestled in the mountains. It is known for the famous Hatfield and McCoy's that were known for their much family feud's. It is also where Patti and I were for a fourth of July "Freedom Festival" in 2012. There was a Tornado that we watched go across the top of the mountain and dropped down in the next village. It tore up trees and downed buildings. It looked somewhat like a war zone. Our tent was upside down, almost a block away. Our tracts were scattered everywhere! The mayor of Logan was a nice man that had his men help us get things put back together. He allowed us to lean the tent against his office building right on the sidewalk. Praise the Lord that He has His people when we need them.

Another place that we do a fair is in Hemlock, NY. We park our camper by Faith Fellowship Church located on Pebble Beach Road in Lakeville, NY. It overlooks Conesus Lake. It is especially nice to watch the sunsets (When we have the chance.). It has a lot of farm country which we like as well as a grape field across the road. The church is about ten years old and the congregation is a very friendly one. Pastor Sweeting is a great preacher/teacher and has done a terrific job for the Lord. His wife went through a horrific health situation. She has recovered wonderfully!

The other great thing about this ministry is that we end up in Florida each year for fairs in that state. We usually arrive at the in November, and leave the middle of May. This keeps us out of the cold up North and able to keep doing our fair ministry. When we are not doing a fair, we usually go Saturday mornings to the local flea markets. The flea market ministry is quite different than the fair booth ministry we usually are involved with. At the flea market we are going to them verses them coming to us. Yet we do have some success at times. One young man I spoke with had just come out of his hedge into a back driveway when a van came rolling out of nowhere and clipped his bike and shoulder. It scraped up his shoulder and bruised him up a bit. I asked him if he knew for sure he would go to heaven when he died. He remembered doing something in the front of a church when he was young. I asked him if he wanted to be sure of going to heaven. Needless to say he now knows Jesus and is sure he is going to heaven!

One of things that we love while in Seffner, Florida is being close to all the Strawberry fields. There is a place close to us that is called Parksdale Strawberry Farm. They are known for their famous "Piled High Strawberry Shortcake." It is a big dish of cake topped with strawberries and whipped crème. Myself, I like the bowl of just strawberries. It is so good. Plus, I probably get more berries this way. There are sometimes a bus loads tourists there. Inside they have pictures of different celebrities and Presidents that have been there. If you are ever in the Seffner/Plant City area of Florida from January through March you need to stop by and have a famous Strawberry Shortcake.

Patti & I would not take anything for the journey that God took us on. We love serving Him and have many wonderful memories. We have seen many wonderful things! We have driven back and forth across America 4 times, and up and down the East coast 8 times now serving our Lord Jesus Christ.

But the greatest thing is to see the face of a person light up, and a big smile when they have accepted Jesus and really meant it!

Thank you Jesus for all you have done! It is an honor to have taken this journey of life from the Unadilla Valley And Beyond, With God!

ABOUT THE BOOK

This is a powerful book of the life of a young boy born in a sharecropper's family when life in the 40's with horses was a struggle. This book will help build a strong family bond. It will encourage, inspire, and give you a greater faith all the while learning that we go through the valleys of life because it is in those times that we can feel the arms of our Jesus hug us, knowing beyond the shadow of doubt He loves us most of all!

You will see that Roy not only had the obstacle of being a sharecroppers son but, also heart surgery; broken neck; and prostate cancer. Yet, through the power of the Holy Spirit he over-came it all and still found time to serve God for over 50 years!

This book will captivate the young and old! Family, friends, and loved ones will enjoy seeing how there is a God in heaven that leads his dear children from birth till death. It is a book of encouragement, and overcoming adversity.

ABOUT THE AUTHOR

The author received his Biblical and Missions training from the Elohim Bible Institute in Castile, New York. He finished his degree work at the Fundamental Baptist Theological Seminary in Youngstown, Ohio. He was a youth pastor for 2 years in Greene, New York. He was a missionary in the Philippines Islands for 10 Years. After recovering from heart surgery he was Principal/Administer for 3 years. He then pastured a small church for 8 years before retiring after breaking his neck and injuring his spine in a fall. After 2 years he felt led to do a senior ministry in his local church for 6 years. The last few years he encourages and counsels people in his local church. He also peer counsels and works as chaplain's assistant in the spinal cord unit at the McGuire Veterans Medical Hospital in Richmond, Virginia. The last 8 plus years he has done Fair and Festival ministries, sharing Christ and leading people to Christ.

He has been state certified by the state of New York in: Bus Driving; all 5 sections of the American Red Cross Disaster program; and is a New York State Court Mediation specialist. He drove bus for the New York State A.R.C. program of Livingston County for 7 years. He and Patti (his lovely wife) have five grown children in various places such as California, Pennsylvania and Michigan. He also has nine grandchildren and 9 great grandchildren. He is pleased that one of his grandsons has also become a foreign missionary. He enjoys traveling and family.

The author is recognized by fellow ministers from Baptist Churches, in New York; Pennsylvania; Texas; West Virginia and Florida. As a Missionary and a Pastor, He has led many people to a saving faith in Jesus Christ and has encouraged many to keep "pressing on the journey for Jesus!"

CPSIA information can be obtained
at www.ICGtesting.com
Printed in the USA
BVHW04s0240120518
516044BV00001B/6/P